PARLIAMENTARY SYSTEM IN INDIA

About the Author

S.G. Deogaonkar has been a teacher and scholar in Political Science for the last thirty-five years. He holds Masters degrees in Political Science and Public Administration and is LL.M in Constitutional Law and Administrative Law. In addition he holds a Ph.D degree in Social Science. His field of specialisation is Constitutional Law, Political Anthropology and Tribal Development. Dr. Deogaonkar has completed many post-doctoral research projects for the U.G.C.and ICSSR and was a National (Post-doctoral) Research Fellow in Tribal Development of the Ministry of Welfare, Government of India. He has participated in numerous conferences and seminars including the Xth International Congress of Anthropological and Ethnological Sciences. He was a Member-Participant of the Socio-Economic Groups on Scheduled Castes and Scheduled Tribes for formulation of the Eighth Five Year Plan Schemes constituted under the Backward Classes Division of the Planning Commission. He is a Non-official Member on the Governing Council of the Tribal Research and Training Institute of the Government of Maharashtra, Pune, and a coopted Member of the Humanities and Social Sciences School of the Yashvantrao Chavan, Maharashtra Open University at Nasik (Maharashtra). He is a member of the Zonal Advisory Board of the Western Zone of the Life Insurance Corporation of India.

Dr. Deogaonkar has published many works like *Administration for Rural Development in India; Political Anthropology; Tribal Exploitation; Tribal Administration and Development; The Banjaras; The Hill Korwas; Tribal Development Plans*, etc.

At present, Dr.Decgaonkar is working as Head, Department of Political Science, at the Anand Niketan College Warora (Maharashtra). Simultaneously, he is also working as an Honorary Chief Research Scientist, at the Centre for Social Science Research on Leprosy, at the Gandhi Memorial Leprosy Foundation at Wardha.

PARLIAMENTARY SYSTEM IN INDIA

S. G. DEOGAONKAR
Head, Department of Political Science
Anand Niketan College
Warora (Maharashtra)

CONCEPT PUBLISHING COMPANY, NEW DELHI-110059

ISBN 81-7022-651-1 (P.B.)

First Published 1997

Published and Printed by
Ashok Kumar Mittal
Concept Publishing Company
A/15-16, Commercial Block, Mohan Garden,
NEW DELHI - 110059 (India)

Phones : 5554042, 5504042
Fax No. : 91-11-5598898

CONTENTS

PREFACE

I am happy to place this book in the hands of my readers. The idea in writing this book was not just to add one more book to the already existing literature on the constitutional government in India, but to write a book on the functioning of the Parliamentary System which has come as a legacy from the British but got institutionalized in the frame created by our Constitution. Later, its functioning was also conditioned by the political and even cultural context prevailing in India, giving us an Indian pattern of the system. This is an endeavour to study and analyse the executive and the legislative branches with emphasis on the details and the intricacies of the functioning of Parliament, the constitutional structures as well as the actual procedures and processes tempering and shaping the practice. Thus, an exploratory review of the evolving structures and processes—both *de jure* and *de facto* forms the core of this study.

Not only inquisitive citizens but even scholars and teachers are likely to be ignorant about the actual functioning of the great democratic institution viz. the Parliament. Here is an attempt to present details about its functioning so that persons can know the various levels of political participation in the making of laws and control of the executive by their representatives and their indirect wielding of power. It is hoped that this will equip them to increase their participation in the democratic process. If they are to respect the structures and abide by their obligations they must first know the processes and their democratic significance.

I must express my deep sense of gratitude towards the 'Bureau of Parliamentary Studies and Training' at the Lok Sabha Secretariat (New Delhi) where I received training, information and material in addition to the views of experts from both the Houses of Parliament on which I could draw upon profusely, so far as the intricate processes are concerned. I must thank them for enlightening me so that I could add valuable information to some chapters.

The original sources with regard to rules and procedure of Lok Sabha Secretariat which were referred included, "Rules of Procedure and Conduct of Business in Lok Sabha," and "Directions by the Speaker". I am extremely thankful to the Secretary-General, Lok Sabha and Deputy Director at the Lok Sabha Secretariat for their advice.

Not only scholars and students but the elite groups who want to know how the democratic institutions work in our democratic republic would find a reading of this book rewarding. Even our budding parliamentarians from the local-self government and Panchayat Raj bodies should find this book useful in knowing and understanding the parliamentary processes.

With these words I conclude this preface, but before that Thank my wife Dr. Shailaja Deogaonkar for her cooperation in my work. I also thank my daughter Advocate Ms. Leena Deogaonkar (now Mrs. Leena A. Baxi) (LL.M. Constitutional law and Administrative Law) for her help and suggestions.

Warora

S.G. DEOGAONKAR

INTRODUCTION

The Ideological Base

The ideological base of the Constitution of India is to be found in the Preamble to the Constitution and in Part IV which gives the principles for the guidance of the future Parliaments, Executives as well as Judiciary. Part III which enumerates the Fundamental Rights also indicates the human, social, economic values that formed the basis for placing the Charter of Rights in the hands of the People of India. It is in the context of these philosophical parameters that one must study and understand the political structures created by the Constitution.

The Preamble

The Preamble has been a matter of pride and praise for Indians, and no less a scholar than Prof. Ernest Barker has mentioned it on the opening page of his famous book *The Principles of Social and Political Theory*. He says,

> "It seemed to me when I read it, to state in a brief and pithy form the argument of much of the book; and it may accordingly serve as a key-note. I am more moved to quote it because I am proud that the People of India should begin their independent life by subscribing to the principles of a political tradition, which we in the West call Western, but which is now something more than Western."[1]

The Preamble indicates the source of the Constitution from which it claims sanction: 'We, the People of India having solemnly resolved do hereby adopt, enact and give to ourselves the Constitution'. Locke said that the People get themselves converted into a 'Sovereign people' by the first part of the social contract and appoint the government by second part of the contract. We are reminded of Locke's theory of social contract while reading the constitutive part of the preamble.

The other aspect of the Preamble is the form or type of State that is created. We have established a 'Sovereign, Democratic Republic 'and the 42nd Amendment added the words 'Socialist, Secular'—adjectives which were ingrained in the original Constitution but were implicit in other provisions and were simply made explicit by the 42nd Amendment.

The objectives mentioned in the Preamble form the most important part of it, and serve as ideological parameters for those who will run the government. These are.

Justice	—	Social, economic and political;
Liberty	—	Of thought, expression, belief, faith and worship;
Equality	—	Of status and of opportunity;
Fraternity	—	Assuring the dignity of the individual and the unity and integrity of the Nation.

These are lofty ideals which form the bases for policy formulation. A question may arise, as to how to operationalise the use of these objectives while framing laws or passing judgments? How can we bring liberty and equality to the thresholds of common masses ?

Parts III and IV of the Constitution provide answer to these questions. Part III gives the Fundamental Rights which are justiciable and contain legal instruments—the writs—for the implementation and protection of these Rights, and Part IV contains the Directive Principles of State Policy, a part with a queer status in so far as it is not justiciable and is not in the form of law though forming an intrinsic part of the fundamental (and supreme) law of the land. This has been framed on the lines of the 'Instruments of Instructions' which appears in the Irish Constitution though the scope in India is different and much wider.

Directive Principles

The principles enumerated in Part IV of Constitution can be broadly divided into four classes viz. economic principles, social principles, political principles and international principles. If implemented—as and when feasible and possible—these can usher in the much needed economic, social and political justice and establish harmonious and peaceful international relations. Quite a few details in all these spheres are enumerated which emphasise social and economic equality for men and women, a socialistic pattern of economy with democratic control, child and mother's care, preserving the capacities of labour, separation of the executive from the judiciary, Panchyati Raj, uniform Civil Code etc. It also insists on the principles of international brotherhood and cooperation, eschewing violence for solving problems, disarmament and much the same policy which later was clubbed under the name *Panchsheel* under Pandit Jawahar Lal Nehru's leadership.

As they stand, the Principles have neither legal status nor force though they have a moral force. As and when the central or state legislature passed laws, these could be implemented. But in the economic field, many laws after enactment had a headlong collision on some fundamental right (more so incase of Right to Property and Right to Liberty) and the cóurts declared them *ultra vires* and hence void. The Parliament went on amending the Constitution to save such laws. This became an unending tug-of-war between Part IIᴵ and laws passed to implement Part IV of the Constitution.

The 25th Constitutional Amendment changed the position. Art. 31(C) gave priority to laws based on these Principles as against the rights in Arts. 14, 19 and 31. The Supreme Court also held the Amendment valid. However, the last and final blow came with the 42nd Amendment enacted in 1976 which gave primacy to laws passed on any of the Directive Principles over Articles 14,19, and 31. Thus any law passed on any of the Principles would not be invalid only because it contravenes the Fundamental Rights in the above Articles. But the Supreme Court did not uphold this amendent as Constitutional. The Court felt that a balance must be struck between the Fundamental Rights and Directive Principles of State Policy and absolute primacy to one over the other should not be given. A harmonious balance must exist, and ideals/objectives ingrained in the Directive Principles should be achieved without abrogating the fundamental rights. In Minerva Mills Ltd. v. Union of India (AIR, 1980, S.C.1789) the expansion of Sec. 31C was held invalid as it destroyed the basic structure of the Constitution by transgressing the limits of amending power. It was held that Part III (Fundamental Rights) and Part IV (Directive Principles) together constitute the core of the Indian Constitution and any attempt 'to destroy the balance between the two will *ipso facto* destroy an essential element of the *basic structure* of the Constitution.

According to political theory, rights and duties are two sides of the same coin. However, in India though Fundamental Rights were given to the citizens, Fundamental Duties were prescribed later, through the 42nd Amendment in 1976.

Fundamental Rights

The *raison d'etre* for the declaration of these rights was the appreciation of the need for securing the welfare of an individual through the fullest development of personality. If citizens are to exercise their will and participate in the democratic processes, some rights become necessary and these must also be guaranteed. Unless there is an egalitarian society there cannot be a real democracy. Indian society was cleavaged through years of foreign rule, both vertically and horizontally. Divisions based on religion, caste, race, class, sex etc. had ravaged the unity of the nation. Economic inequalities and oppressions were rampant. Hence, a few rights which were recognized as vital for socio-economic, political and religious life were guaranteed under Part III of the Constitution and were made justiciable. They have been protected from the encroachment of the State. Laws made in contravention of these rights are void. This position was confirmed by the Supreme Court in Minerva Mills Case (1980).

These rights are—

(1) Right to Equality (Arts.14, 15, and 16, 17, 18).
(2) Right to Freedom (Arts.19–22).
(3) Right against Exploitation (Arts. 23, 24).
(4) Right to Freedom of Religion (Arts. 25–28).
(5) Cultural and Educational Rights (Arts. 29, 30).
(6) Right to Property (Arts. 31 to 31C).
(Deleted by 44th Amendment).
(7) Right to Constitutional Remedies (Arts. 32 to 35).

Right to Equality

It establishes equality before the law which ensures the rule of law and equal protection of laws to all citizens. Social equality irrespective of race, religion, caste, sex etc. at all public places and equality of opportunity in matters of employment is also assured. Abolition of untouchability and abolition of titles is also a part of this right.

Right to Freedom

The seven freedoms guaranteed include:

(a) freedom of speech and expression ,

(b) right to assemble peaceably and without arms,
(c) right to form associations or unions,
(d) right to reside and settle in any part of the territory of India,
(e) to acquire, hold and dispose of property (Deleted by the 44th Amendment and made a legal right), and
(f) right to practise any profession, or to carry on any occupation, trade or business.

All these freedoms are tempered with exceptions and limits in the context security and integrity of India, social cohesion and morality and limits imposed by other laws etc.

Protection to life and personal liberty has been assured and these cannot be taken away except according to procedure established by law. In Maneka Gandhi v. Union of India (1978) the Supreme Court has held that such procedure must be reasonable, fair and just and not arbitrary. The exceptions were provided by preventive detention (e.g. under MISA,TADA etc.) but its scope is circumscribed by the 44th Amendment. Self-incrimination and double jeopardy are also eliminated.

Right Against Exploitation

This right prohibits traffic in human beings and forced labour of all types like *Begar* etc. Compulsory service for public purposes can be taken by State without discriminating on the basis of religion, race, caste etc.

Right to Freedom of Religion

Considering the secular nature of our State and the historical happenings, this right assumed special significance. All persons are equally entitled to freedom of conscience and to freely profess, practise and propagate the religion subject to the provisions of public order, morality and health etc. No person can be compelled to accept any particular creed or practice of religion. Sikhs are permitted to use *Kirpans* without offending the law. Every religious denomination can establish and maintain institutions for religious and charitable purposes; to manage its own affairs in matters of religion; to own and acquire movable and immovable property and to administer such property. The attitude of state to religion is supposed to be neutral except regulatory functions to avoid conflict or public unrest. Compulsory religious instruction in educational institutions maintained by the state or recognized or aided by the state is prohibited.

Cultural and Educational Rights

This right assures protection to minorities speaking different languages and scripts. Any section of citizens residing in any part of India having a distinct language, script or culture of its own has a right to conserve the same. No minority shall be discriminated against in matters of admission to any educational institution maintained or aided by state. They can establish and administer educational institutions. Their language script and culture are also recognized and protected.

Right to Property Deleted by 44th Amendment

Here the intention was to delete it as a fundamental right and not as a legal right. Hence Art. 300A was inserted (in Part XII) which states that "No person shall be deprived of his property save by authority of law."

Right to Constitutional Remedies

This is an effective and easy remedy for enforcing these rights. This right entrusts the responsibility for enforcement of these rights to the Supreme Court (Art. 32) and the High Courts, (Art. 226). The Courts can issue directions or orders or writs in the nature of *habeas corpus, mandamus, prohibition, quo-warranto* and *certiorari*. A citizen whose right is encroached upon may, through an appropriate petition move the court and pray the court for the issue of appropriate writ to enforce the right.

Habeas corpus, a landmark in protection of liberty, provides a remedy against wrongful confinement, detention and thus secures personal liberty. *Mandamus* is a high prerogative writ of extensive remedial nature for compelling any public authority/individual or Court to perform act falling under its duty. While *Prohibition* prevents any transgression of jurisdiction by a Court or quasi-judicial authority, *Certiorari* remedies any such excess of jurisdiction or function. *Quo-warranto* can question the claim to any office or franchise and helps in determination of the proper claim or right to such office, franchise etc.

The Fundamental Rights have been circumscribed by various exception, provisos, limits and prohibitions, some directed against the person(s) who enjoy these rights, and also against the Parliament,

Union Government, State legislatures and State governments and other authorities. Nevertheless, the rights have proved to be real and effective and citizens have exercised them. Judiciary has been vigilant and whenever moved has very ably enforced these rights, even invalidating Acts of Parliament and fighting Constitutional battles to protect them. The spirit of the Courts is vindicated in cases like the Gopalan case, Golaknath case, Keshavananda Bharti case, Maneka Gandhi case and the Minerva Mills case. On the whole the ideals and objects accepted and enshrined in our Constitution have been brought to reality through the actions of legislature and the executive and the judiciary supporting and or controlling these two in the light of the basic philosophy and structure of the Constitution.

Fundamental Duties

These were introduced in the Constitution through the 42nd Amendment. They are:

51A: It shall be the duty of every citizen of India:

(A) to abide by the Constitution and respect its ideals and institutions, the National Flag and the National Anthem;
(B) to cherish and follow the noble ideals which inspired our national struggle for freedom;
(C) to uphold and protect the sovereignty, unity and integrity of India;
(D) to defend the country and render national service when called upon to do so;
(E) to promote harmony and the spirit of common brotherhood amongst all the people of India transcending religious, linguistic and regional or sectional diversities; to renounce practices derogatory to the dignity of women;
(F) to value and preserve the rich heritage of our composite culture;
(G) to protect and improve the natural environment including forests, lakes, rivers and wild life; and to have compassion for living creatures;
(H) to develop the scientific temper, humanism and the spirit of inquiry and reform;
(I) to safeguard public property and to abjure violence;
(j) to strive towards excellence in all spheres of individual and collective activity, so that the nation constantly rises to higher levels of endeavour and achievement.

Apart from being vague in meaning and scope, these fundamental duties are not linked with the enjoyment of fundamental rights, nor is there any mention regarding the provision of their enforcement. As it stands, these don't seem to be justiciable. However, they add a few more values and ideals to the list of lofty ideals to be kept before the Indian citizens as well as those who are entrusted with the job of running our "Sovereign, Socialist, Secular, Democratic Republic".

REFERENCE

1. Barker Ernest, 1961:*The Principles of Social and Political Theory,* Oxford University Press, London, p. vi.

1

THE EXECUTIVES OF THE UNION

India i.e. Bharat is a sovereign, democratic republic and opted for parliamentary form of government as legacy from Great Britain which is considered a Mother of parliamentary democracy. However, the rise and growth of the parliamentary government in Britain has been an evolutionary process, evolved through historical events and to a large extent a product of 'chance and wisdom' (Anson). The principles and practices laying down the basis of parliamentary government are born out of customs and conventions which enjoy unstinted support of the British public opinion and ensures their strict and meticulous observation—bordering on ritualism—and any break in these traditions may invite public wrath threatening revolution. This political conservatism is the cement which has provided firm moorings to the flexible constitutionalism, based on an evolved, unwritten, non-documentary constitution which consists of heterogene-ous elements such as Treaties, Charters etc., the Statutes or Acts of Parliament, judicial decisions, Common Law and last but the most important than these written and quasi-written parts, the costums, traditions, usages and conventions. It is this last element viz. customs, usages and conventions which forms the basis of the parliamentary government including the titularity of the King (and the institution of Crown), the requirement of summoning the Parliament at least once in an year, the Cabinet and the Ministry, its responsibility and answerability to the House of Commons, joint collective responsibility of the Ministry, the position of the Prime Minister, etc. The historical changes which rendered the erstwhile all-powerful, hereditary Kingship titular, and transferred all powers to the "Convenient working hypothesis"(Sidney Low) the Crown, which is an institutionalised Kingship, the rise of the House of Lords from *Magnum concilium,* the rise of the House of

Commons, the growth of the strength of the Commons and depletion in the powers of the Lords, the rise of the Ministry, the office of the Prime Minister, the Cabinet, Inner cabinets etc. and the pivotal role of the Prime Minister and many other structures are not born out of any written statute but primarily from customs and conventions, which, through years of popular support, crystallized into constitutional structures. Of late a few have been recognised and/or consolidated through Acts of Parliament and recognized and implemented by Courts, thus finding place in the Common law . The Ministers of the Crown Act (1937) and the rights of British citizens are examples respectively.

Though India had some structures simulating the British ones before Independence, they were just hollow so far as their real powers and representative character were concerned. It was only after the Indian Constitution came into effect that the real democratic and parliamentary structures started operating in our political system.

Thus, a federal form of government with a nominal head—President (termed as *Rashtrapati* in our Constitution) with a Council of Ministers with the Prime Minister at the head, to aid and advise the President in the exercise of his functions was created. The basic departure from the British Constitution was that, (i) while the British parliamentary form was a creation of tradition and convention, the Indian pattern has had its origin the articles of a written Constitution, and (ii) while the British nominal head has been a hereditary office with a historical background, the Indian nominal head is an elected office for a fixed term. All executive power is vested in the President and executive actions are taken in his name, however, as he is a nominal head, the real exercise of power rests with the Council of Ministers which, in fact, is the Political Executive drawing its support from the Parliament.

The President is elected by a special electoral college consisting of all the elected members of *Lok Sabha* and *Rajya Sabha* and the elected members from the *Vidhan Sabhas* of the states. The election is by single transferable vote system so as to ensure proportional representation. An elaborate formula which considers the population of a State as the basis, is prescribed to calculate the numerical value of the vote cast by each member of this electoral college. All disputes regarding the President's election are settled by the Supreme Court. He can be removed for violation of Constitution only by Impeachment which needs framing of charges in one of the Houses of Parliament by a special majority (two-thirds majority of votes of the present and voting members and absolute majority of the total membership of the House) and ratification in the other House by special majority after giving him an opportunity to defend himself. A notice signed by not less than one-fourth of the total membership of the Houses which will frame the charges ought to be given in writing at least fourteen days in advance. Thus his office is made very safe and he cannot be removed on flimsy grounds.

The President enjoys many powers which are broadly classified as under:

(i) Executive powers,
(ii) Legislative powers,
(iii) Financial powers,
(iv) Judicial powers,
(v) Emergency powers.

However, impressive the list of powers and their sweep may be, he being a nominal head, these are enjoyed by the Council of Ministers headed by the Prime Minister. The 42nd Amendment (1976) added the words '. . . and that the President shall abide by such advice'. Thus what was implicit was made explicit; without materially changing the position. The 44th Amendments added that the President may require the Council of Ministers to reconsider the advice given by it, and the President shall act on such advice tendered after such reconsideration. The sum-total of all such provisions is that he remains a nominal head with statutory powers only to ask for a reconsideration. This position makes all the powers of the Council of Ministers—with in fact the President giving advice which may or may not be accepted.

The Executive Powers*

The Executive powers of the President include the appointment of the Prime Minister and the Union Council of Ministers, distribution of portfolios, though such appointments are a formality, the real process depending upon the majority the Lok Sabha.

He appoints the Attorney-General, Comptroller and Auditor- General, Chief Justice and Puisne justices of the Supreme Court and High Courts, the Chief Election Commissioner, India's Ambassadors and representatives in foreign countries/International bodies, Chairman and Member of the Union Public Service Commission, Governors of States, Chief Commissioners of Union Territories. He is the Com-

* The term 'Executive' has been used in Art 73 (1) of the Constitution and is used here to indicate the political executive including the Council of Ministers, while 'administrative' should refer to permanent services or the administrative machinery.

mander-in-Chief of all the three Defence Forces and as such appoints the Chiefs-of-Staff of the Army, Navy and Air Force. He can declare war and sign treaties. In reality all these functions are performed by the Council of Ministers though the signature and seal is that of the President. He receives the credentials of Ambassadors accredited to India by other countries—something that he physically does himself. That way he personally presides over all ceremonial occasions representing or symbolising the dignity, integrity and sovereignty of the nation.

Legislative Powers

The President is a part and parcel of the Parliament *(Sansad)* as on bill passed by the Parliament can become a Law without his signature. He summons, adjourns and prorogues the session of Parliament and if required can summon extraordinary session. He delivers the opening speech at the 1st session which is called *Rashtrapati's Abhibhashan* (President's Inaugural Speech), which, as per the Parliamentary tradition, is drafted by the Prime Minister, though read out by the President. He can call a joint sitting of both Houses of Parliament and can send messages to the Houses. In particular circumstances, he may dissolve Lok Sabha.

As far as the constitution of the Houses is concerned, he may appoint two Anglo-Indians to Lok Sabha if not elected through elections. Similarly, he can nominate twelve persons to Rajya Sabha from among such persons who have rendered outstanding services in the field of literature, science, art and social service.

As for the legislative functions of the Parliament, certain bills like money bills or bills seeking to change name(s) or boundaries of state(s) can not be introduced in Parliament without his prior consent. In case of ordinary bill, after it is passed by both the Houses of Parliament, it is sent for his assent. The President may give his assent in which case it becomes a Law—or may return it with or without reasons/suggestions. In such cases it must be reconsidered by both the Houses as per requirements of the Constitution. However, if the Parliament passes it again in the same form and sends it to him for the second time for his assent the Constitution provides that, 'the President shall not withhold his assent'. Thus it becomes incumbent on him to give his assent.

In certain cases the President may keep the bill pending with him for a long time as any specific time limit has not been prescribed. Thus a sort of suspensive veto may be applied. In fact in the scheme, as envisaged in our Constitution, an absolute veto does not exist.(And naturally should not exist as we have a parliamentary form of government). But certain political changes at the level of Ministry may, in fact, lead to a situation when a suspensive veto may turn out to be an absolute veto. Some authors have also fancied to maintain that the President in India has a *Pocket-Veto,* but it does not exist in the sense it is operative in the United States of America. (For a detailed discussion on this point please refer to Chapter 3, p. 94).

President can promulgate ordinances on all subjects on which the parliament has powers to legislate. He may issue an ordinance when the Parliament is not in session and he is convinced that circumstances exist which render it necessary to act. Such an ordinance must be laid before both the Houses of Parliament and should be ratified within six weeks from the re-assembly of Parliament. If it is not ratified by the Parliament it ceases to operate. As and when an Ordinance is in force it shall be operated like any other law of Parliament and have the same force as law. This power is a relic of the powers of the Governor-General in the pre-Republic era.

Certain bills passed by the State legislatures may be sent by the Governor for President's assent. If he returns the bill and it is passed and sent to him in the same form for second time he may still refuse assent in which case the bill is killed! Thus he has an absolute veto power in case of state bills.

Financial Powers

No money bill can be introduced in parliament without President's prior consent. The annual budget is presented by the Finance Minister on his behalf. His permission is necessary for adding to or spending from the Consolidated Fund of India. He operates the Contingency Fund and can sanction money for unexpected and unforeseen calamities etc. In fact all these 'permissions' mean a sanction of Parliament and the consent of the President to the bill sanctioning such transactions.

The President is required to appoint a Finance Commission after every five years consisting of a Chairman and four other members which makes recommendations on the distribution of the proceeds of Income Tax and certain other taxes between the Union and the States and lays down principles on the basis of which the grants-in-aid of revenues of the States from the Consolidated Fund of India are to be governed. The recommendations of the Commission and the action taken on them are to be laid before the Parliament by the President. This is an important function of the President as head of a federal structure.

Judicial Powers

With a view to keep the Judiciary free from interference and independent, only such powers and functions are entrusted to the President which pertain to the constituting of Courts and/or after the judicial procedure is over. Thus, he appoints the Chief Justice of the Supreme Court, Chief Justices of the High Courts and other judges of the Supreme Court and High Courts. He also decides the number of judges of these Courts. His consent is necessary for removal of a judge though the Parliament, by special majority in both Houses, recommends the removal of a judge. The President has powers of pardon, reprieve, amnesty, mercy and/or reduction in punishment which may be exercised as head of the Union, and only after all judicial remedies are over. However, this extends only to offences coming under the executive power of the Union.

Emergency Powers

Of late there had been a feeling that a federal form of government, though a useful contrivance to achieve national unity and regional autonomy, proves a weak form during emergencies. Probably, the framers of the Constitution kept these emergency provisions as the corrective on this probable weakness. This special feature of our Constitution is the way in which the normal, peace-time federalism can be adapted to emergency conditions.

The President enjoys these powers under three types of emergencies:

(i) A threat to the security of India or any part thereof whether by war or external aggression or armed rebellion,
(ii) failure of constitutional machinery in a state,
(iii) financial emergency.

The proclamation of emergency by a President is warranted only under exceptional circumstances, and is not to be used as a political weapon.

Before 1978, the expression 'internal disturbance' was there in the first category, but so as to exclude any probability of declaration on flimsy grounds the 44th Amendment substituted the words 'armed rebellion'. Moreover, the President is supposed to make the proclamation only on the advice of the ministry which would be sufficient for him to get himself 'satisfied' about the existence of grave emergency. The 44th Amendment introduced a clause providing that

President shall not declare emergency, unless the decision of the Union Cabinet that such a proclamation may be issued has been communicated to him in writing. Thus, the Prime Minister alone cannot tender such advice, but has to be arrived at collectively by the Cabinet. Parliament must approve such proclamation within one month (previously it was two months) in both Houses, failing which it ceases to operate. If at the time of declaration the Lok Sabha is dissolved, the Rajya Sabha must approve it and the new Lok Sabha must approve it within 30 days after its sitting begins, failing which the proclamation ceases to operate. Similarly, before the 44th Amendment, simple majority in both the Houses was enough for approval, but the 44th Amendment provided for a majority of the total membership and not less than two-thirds majority of the members present and voting in each House. This equates the approval to an amendment of the Constitution; and provides a foolprof safeguard against improvident use of the provision. Once approved, it remains for six months, unless revoked earlier by the President. Thus, after every six months Parliament can review the proclamation. (Previously the executive could prolong the declaration upto three years).

In case of failure of the Constitutional machinery in a State the President may invoke his emergency powers and proclaim a state of emergency in that State on receipt of a report from the Governor of the State or otherwise, if satisfied that a situation has arisen in which the Government of a State cannot be carried on in accordance with the provisions of the Constitution. In such cases, by proclamation, the President assumes functions of the State Government, the State Ministry is suspended and the Governor runs the administration in the capacity of the President's representative. He may even dissolve the State legislature or keep it in an animated suspension and may declare that the powers of the State legislature may be exercised by Parliament during the period of proclamation. The proclamation must be approved by Parliament—both Houses—within two months failing which it ceases operate. This continues for six months after which a fresh proclamation with fresh approval is necessary, thus providing for periodical review. The President's Rule may be continued for a maximum of three years after which the normal constitutional machinery in the State must be restored.

This provision has been used by the Union Governments as political weapon against a ministry in a State from a rival party or group.

Financial crisis envisages unstable economic conditions in the country. If the President is satisfied that a situation has arisen in which financial stability or credit of India is threatened, he may by proclamation declare to that effect. Parliament's approval in necessary within two months. Such a declaration may have the effect of reducing the salaries, allowances of services in the Union, States, Judges of Supreme Court or High Court. Money bills, even from the States, may be required to get assent of the President. Allocation of revenue between the Union and States may be changed during the period.

President's Position

An overview of all the above powers of the President depicts a picture of a really powerful head of the State, which is not true. Allen Gladhill was led to argue that by skilfully using various provisions, the President can become a virtual dictator. However, these are far-stretched ideas incompatible with the spirt as well as provisions of the Constitution which create a nominal head under a parliamentary system.

Is the President as nominal as the British Monarch? He has the power to 'advise, encourage and warn the Ministers in respect of the recommendations that they make'. The following provisions as they stand after the 44th Amendment present a particular picture.

(1) He can require the Council of Ministers to reconsider the advice tendered (Art. 74 (1)).
(2) Right to be informed about the country's affairs (Art. 78) and it is the duty of the Prime Minister to keep him informed, and to furnish such information as the President may call for (Art. 78(b)).
(3) The President may require the Prime Minister to submit any matter on which a decision has already been taken for a reconsideration by the Council of Ministers. This assures the principle of collective responsibility as against the probable high-handedness of Prime Ministers.

The above provisions indicate that the President is not an absolutely non-effective, nominal head.

However, one must also remember that:

(1) . . . the President shall act in accordance with such advice tendered after such reconsideration (by the Council of Ministers).
(2) The Courts cannot enquire into what advice, if any, has been given by the Ministers to the President (Art. 74(2)). It is protected from disclosure.

In cases where the President may not abide by such advice the only recourse can be the impeachment of the President and this being a difficult procedure is possible only if the Council of Ministers enjoys necessary majority in both the Houses.

Similarly, when there is an absolute majority of one party in Lok Sabha and they elect their leader, the President has no option but to appoint the person as Prime Minister and on his advice, the other Ministers. But in cases when no single party enjoys an absolute majority and different parties/groups claim to form government, it is President's discretion to select a Prime Minister from among the rival claimants. The only objective criterion which he is supposed to apply is, who can form a (at least relatively) stable government. This is one of the functions in which he has to use his discretion, without the 'aid and advice' of the Ministry which is not in existence. Only factual position of parties and the requirement of a stable government are his guide lines. During the Ninth and the Tenth Lok Sabha (1989, 1991 and 1996) such occasions arose, in view of the so-called hung-Parliaments.

Similarly, on the defeat of a ministry in Lok Sabha, two options are open to the Prime Minister—he may either tender resignation of his Ministry or advise the President to dissolve the House (Lok Sabha) and order fresh mandate from the people i.e. elections (ostensibly claiming that though the confidence of people's representatives has been lost, the Council still enjoys the trust of the people and as such they would again be returned to power with full majority). However, it is again in the President's discretion and judgment whether to accept the advice and dissolve the House and seek a fresh mandate from the people or to give an opportunity to other party/group in the House to form a Ministry. This power and discretion of the President is— obviously—outside 'the advice' of the Prime Minister and his Council which has lost majority support.

Thus, the Constitutional and legal basis and power behind a Ministry is, in fact, drawn from the support of the majority in the Lok Sabha, and all his (Prime Minister's) *de facto* as well as *de jure* constitutional status vi-a-vis the President is based on it. As soon as he loses this support and the political scene gets uncertain and fluid, the nominal head—the President—becomes a real head and uses his discretion, till he again establishes a stable Council of Ministers with a stable and full support in the House. When no single political party has majority to sustain a Council of Ministers on its own strength, the position of the President would be slightly more powerful having a see-saw relationship, marginalising the position of the Prime Minister.

He (the President) is not as nominal as the British Monarch as he can return a Bill to the Parliament for reconsideration which the British Monarch has ceased to do since Queen Ann returned the Scottish Militia Bill (1707 A.D.). The President's position cannot be fully equated to that of the British Monarch for the following reasons:

(1) The President is an elected head of our Republic.

(2) He has powers given by a written Constitution which is the supreme law of the land (thus modifying the British concept of the Sovereignty of the Parliament).

(3) He is heading a Federal structure and as such has to perform functions which are concerned with the interests of the State governments (e.g. he may return a Bill of State legislature for the second time in which case it is 'killed'). Especially when the party in power at the Center is different than that of in a State, and due to political rivalry and strife, the Council of Ministers recommends an action which is obviously unopportune and unwarranted except on political considerations, will it be still binding on the President to act accordingly and get 'satisfied' about the necessity of the action without thinking about the bona fides and intentions of the 'advice'? He is head of the Federal structure and while the Council of Ministers and the Prime Minister are responsible to and removable by the Lok Sabha alone by simple majority, the President can be removed only when both the Houses impeach him by special majority. Thus, the Rajya Sabha which is the care-taker of the interest of the States must also concur with the Lok Sabha. This shows that the Constitution has tacitly recognised President's status not only as head of the Central government but also of the Union i.e. including the States in our federal polity. The above points do make a difference between the position of the British Monarch and the Indian President, the later being less nominal than the former.

Though there is no provision in our Constitution regarding the total number of terms for which a person can work as President, the precedent has been of two terms.

Shri M.V. Pylee rightly mentions the occasions on which the President's discretion is operative in this regard. "First, when no party in the Parliament i.e. precisely House of the People has a clear majority—or a multitude of small parties in Parliament, none capable of forming a stable Ministry.....an ambitious President may dictate terms..... Secondly, the majority party which holds the reins of power is torn asunder by internal disputes and dissensions.... when discipline in the ruling party degenerates, when groups and factions undermine party cohesion, when adventurous and unscrupulous group-bosses try to capture office through questionable means, and, finally, when corrupt practices tarnish the reputation and goodwill of the ruling party, there will be an opportunity for the President to play a decisive role in the machinery of the Government. In the ultimate analysis, it is the political climate that will dictate the use of his power"[1]. Analysing the political scenario during 1992-93 and during 1996-97 may help in appreciating the above analysis.

The President of the Indian Republic is an elected President, derives his powers from a written Constitution and is Head of a federal polity. Hence unlike his British counterpart he occupies a different position which certainly makes his position less nominal. During Rajiv Gandhi's Prime Ministership, the then President Gyani Zail Singh's letter caused a political storm over his relationship with the Prime Minister and ultimately the Prime Minister in spite of the majority support in the House, started visiting the President and keeping him 'informed'. Thus the 'nominal' head in our Parliamentary System can become powerful to match the exigencies of the political expediency. He cannot be just ignored in all situations.

The Vice-President

The Vice-President is elected by the electoral college consisting of the elected Members of Lok Sabha and rajya Sabha, by Single Transferable Vote System under the methods of proportional representation. All disputes regarding his election are referred to and decided by the Supreme Court. He holds office for five years.

The Vice-President of India is the *ex-officio* Chairman of Rajya Sabha and his usual function is to conduct the business of the House. But he cannot vote as he is not a Member of that House. He may cast his casting vote.

If the President is away from the country, or on tour, or is ill and hence unable to attend to his office the Vice-President shall discharge the functions of the President. If the President's post falls vacant due to death, resignation or impeachment of the President, the Vice-President shall discharge his functions and shall assume full powers. However, this arrangement can continue for six months. Before the expiry of this period electing a new President is necessary.

The Vice-President may be removed from office by a resolution passed in Rajya Sabha and agreed to by Lok Sabha, but 14 day's notice is necessary for moving such resolution.

The Council of Minister

In India, unlike in Britain, the Council of Ministers is a product of the Constitution. Article 53(1) states that the executive power of the Union is vested in the President, and shall be exercised by him either *directly or through officers subordinate to him* in accordance with this Constitution. Article 74(1) stated (before the 42nd Amendment) that 'there shall be a Council of Ministers with the *Prime Minister at the head to* aid and advise the President in the exercise of his functions (42nd Amendment added) and that the President shall act in accordance with such advice in the discharge of his functions.' Thus, a thing which was implicit was made explicit. The 44th Amendment further provided that the President may ask the Ministry to reconsider, but shall act in accordance with advice tendered after such reconsideration.

In fact, the real function of the President is to appoint the Prime Minister who selects his Ministers and distributes their portfolios, which is formally declared under the President's signature and seal. Hence though the Parliamentary system is the same as in Britain the basis here is a constitutional one written in specific words. After general elections, the party which obtains an absolute majority in the Lok Sabha elects its leader whose name is sent to the President and a claim to form a government is put forth. In such cases, like the British Monarch, the President has no option but to invite him to form a Ministry. But in a situation in which no party has got an absolute majority and more than one party or a conglomerate of splinter-groups put forth rival claims to form government under the leadership of their leader(s) in the House, the President's discretion assumes real significance. Such a situation arose after the elections held in 1989 and 1991 i.e. in the Ninth and Tenth Lok Sabha respectively. The Eleventh Lok Sabha in 1996 saw an unprecedented scene of 13 antagonistic parties coming together to form a United Front Government. Political promises based on bargaining formed the basis of the promised support (whether from outside i.e. remaining out of the Ministry but supporting on the floor of the Houses or from within i.e. by joining the government) which may or may not last longer. It is for the President to decide as to which claimant can assure a (relatively) stable government. Need for a stable government is the only criterion on which the President ought to exercise his discretion.

The Council of Ministers and Cabinet

In the Indian Constitution the term used is the Council of Ministers. The word Cabinet has been adopted from the British vocabulary and practice. The Prime Minister designates some Ministers as full-fledged Ministers and they form the Cabinet. Normally the Ministers incharge of important portfolios like Finance, Home, Defence, Foreign Affairs etc. are Cabinet Ministers. However, the Prime Minister's confidants, important leaders in the party, leaders heading influencial groups in the party etc. are also given this status. Cabinet Minister is only a status which enables the Minister to attend all cabinet meeting as a matter of right. Others are designated as Ministers of State, who are in some Ministry with a Cabinet Minister or may even head a Ministry independently. A Minister of State can attend meetings of Cabinet only he is specially invited to attend the same. The Deputy Minister is a subordinate Minister who assists a Cabinet Minister or Minister of State and thus has a subordinate status. This *three-tier* system as it is called these days—is a product of convention and practice and has no constitutional basis.

The Council of Ministers rarely meets. The Prime Minister convenes the meeting of Cabinet which may also be attended by Ministers who are not of cabinet rank but are invited to attend. The Prime Minister prepares the agenda and presides over the meeting. The cabinet deliberates and decides on all policy matters—of all Departments and takes decisions on all important matters. The meetings are secret and Members can express their views freely and there is a discussion on all points. Decisions are taken either by consensus or by voting, but the Prime Minister's views exert a lot of influence on all decisions. Once a decision is taken it is binding not only on the Cabinet Ministers but on all Ministers in the Council of Ministers including the Ministers of State and Deputy Ministers. All must support it and defend it, both within and out side the Parliament, and those who are not ready to reconcile with the decision must resign and come out of the Ministry. This is essential for maintaining the collective responsibility of the Council of Minister.

A Minister ought to be a Member of either of the Houses and if not, he must get elected to the House within six months, failing which he shall not continue as a Minister. This is the only constitutional restriction, others being political in nature. The Prime Minister tries to give presentation to all parts of India, States, communities etc. and last but not the least the groups and factions in his own party. As aptly said in Britain the qualities of a successful minister must be,

"........resourceful, a superman, knowledge of public affairs, able to think straight and to express himself clearly on the floor of the Parliament, quick in decision—and at least half the times right, able to sift gook advice from bad when he hears it." The confidants of the Prime Minister do find a berth in the Ministry.

Collective Responsibility

Ministers are collectively responsible to the Parliament. Apart from Article 74, the following provisions usher in the Parliamentary form (Art.75):

(1) The Prime Minister shall be appointed by the President and the other Ministers shall be appointed by the President on the advice of the Prime Minister.
(2) The Ministers shall hold office during the pleasure of the President.
(3) The Council of Ministers shall be collectively responsible to the House of the People.
(4) A Minister who is not a member of either House of Parliament for six months shall cease to be a Minister after expiration of six months.
(5) The salaries and allowances of Ministers be determined by law by Parliament from time to time.

All the above provisions unequivocally point towards a parliamentary system. The term 'pleasure of the President' raised doubts in the minds of some Members of the Constituent assembly. Explaining the provision Dr. Ambedkar said—

> "one ground on which a Minister could be liable of dismissal would be that he has lost confidence of the House. Secondly, that his administration is not pure, because the word used here is 'pleasure'. The President may call for the removal of a particular Minister on the ground that he is guilty of corruption or bribery or mal-administration, although he enjoys the confidence of the House. The two conditions that govern the tenure of a Minister in office are purity of administration and confidence of the House."

Thus, the Council of Ministers carved out from the majority party's Members in the Parliament is a part and parcel of the house and survives till it enjoys the confidence of the Parliament. In reality the 'pleasure' is of the Parliament than that of the President except in cases of impurity when he can dismiss a Minister. (But usually this is done on the advice of the Prime Minister, or in most of the cases the Prime Minister advises the concerned Minister to resign.)

The collective responsibility is possible when there is homogeneity —meaning particularly political homogeneity and oneness or uniformity of approach in policy and one-leadership viz. of the Prime Minister. In India it has been observed time and again that when there were formidable rivals for Prime Ministership, a Deputy Prime Minister's post was created and such governments could not function for long. In Smt. Indira Gandhi's Ministry, Morarji Desai was Deputy Prime Minister but then not only the Ministry but the Congress Party itself gave way. Similarly, during the Janata Government's regime, Morarji Desai was the Prime Minister and Chaudhari Charan Singh was the Deputy Prime Minister when the same thing happened. The latest example was seen after the 1989 general elections when the minority government headed by V.P. Singh as the Prime Minister with Devilal as Deputy Prime Minister, also did not survive for long. This indicates that single leadership of the Prime Minister is essential to maintain the solidarity as well as collective responsibility of the Ministry.

Answerability

The Ministry stands together or falls together. Every Minister is answerable for the Department he heads and is also collectively responsible for the policy adopted by the Cabinet. This responsibility and answerability towards Parliament is functionalised. The Ministry is presumed to have lost confidence if:

(1) A Prestigious Bill introduced by the Ministry fails to get majority support and is lost particularly in the Lok Sabha, or a Bill opposed by the Ministry is passed.
(2) A Money Bill is disapproved and cuts if any to the Budget are introduced by the House.
(3) A censure motion is passed against one or more Ministers.
(4) A no-confidence motion is passed against a Ministry in the Lok Sabha.

As per the British practice adopted in India acceptance of an Adjournment motion for discussion in the House is also a strong censure of the Government but for this the Ministry may not resign. (discussed at length in Chapter 3).

Question Hour also helps a thorough screening of the failures of Ministries and is almost a cross-examination of the Minister who is under a Parliamentary obligation to give proper, correct and detailed answers. The Speaker can warn a Minister giving vague answers or evading answers and compel him to provide proper information. Some information may be withheld in national or public interest. This hour influences general public opinion and hence, though it does not invite resignation of the Minister, it is taken seriously by them. Since live telecast on Television, the impact on public opinion has increased.

In all cases wherein the Ministry loses the confidence of the Parliament (practically that of the Lok Sabha) the Ministry resigns. The other option open in for the Prime Minister to advise the President to dissolve the Lok Sabha and order fresh elections (the presumption being that his ministry expects the support of the people). However, it is purely in the President's discretion to accept this advice or not. He may call other party's/group's leader in the House to form a Ministry.

The Prime Minister

Like Great Britain, the Indian Prime Minister is also 'the key-stone of the Cabinet arch'.

In Britain his position has evolved through chance, custom and convention and he is supposed to be *primus inter pares* i.e. first among equals i.e. first in the ministry. This gives him priority, or leadership, but in any sense is not superior or a 'boss'. In India, as stated earlier the article states '. . . there shall be a Council of Ministers with the *Prime Minister at the head'* and as this is *written* in the Constitution his position cannot be called strictly as that of 'first among equals' but may be correctly described as 'the head of the equals'. It is he who select his colleagues, distributes portfolios among them, advises the President to dismiss a particular Minister, calls and presides over the meetings of the Cabinet and mostly *leads* it to a decision. He irons out differences amidst ministers and strikes coordination which is necessary to maintain collective responsibility. He leads the Ministry in the House and is its chief spokesman particularly in all important debates and discussions. He is also the Leader of the House as he is the leader of the parliamentary party having majority in the House. He is the person having a total view and knowledge of the administration as a whole and supervises the working of Ministers. He is the chief and the only link between the President and the Ministry as well as the President and Parliament. He is duty bound to keep the President informed about the latest position, policies and actions of his government. He also must carry the President's 'advice' to his Ministry and convene its meeting for reconsideration on that basis (which may or may not revise its decision).

The Prime Ministers in India have also been selected from the Lok Sabha and as such, this has become a convention. It is also essential for assuring his answerability towards Lok Sabha. Some incumbents to the post were not members of Parliament at all but were elected within six months. Shri P.V Narasimha Rao (1991) is the latest example. Later he was elected to the House creating a record of votes polled.

In spite of a strong political and popular backing to the parliamentary form that we adopted and the express Constitutional provisions as detailed above (Arts. 74, 75), the Cabinet and the Prime Minister have tended to become more powerful leading to a situation which, in Britain, is described as Cabinet dictatorship. This was partly due to the personality and behaviour of the First Prime Minister, who was a *chairsma* for the people of India and for the Indian National Congress which was the only party having maximum national following. He had a firm and undeterred will-power, tremendous capacities, a vision and enjoyed full faith and confidence of the people. Legal-institutional and chrismatic authority were combined in him. Later, Lal Bahadur Shastri also provided a firm and strong leadership (though for a brief span) which was morally strong and towering. Indira Gandhi, who, when she came to power as Prime Minister, was described by some political rivals as a 'dumb doll' had all the three types of Max Weber's 'authority' combined in her viz. traditional authority, (Nehru family), legal-institutional and charismatic authority. When she took over she had told the press, "My father (Nehru) was saint, I am not; I *mean* to *rule*". And she kept her promise right upto the roots of her word and made 'dumb' all those rivals who had described her as a dumb doll. She had the guts to advise the President to declare emergency and then call a meeting of her cabinet colleagues and to get it okayed by them without grumbling. Morarji Desai, Prime Minister under the short-lived Janata Party government, was also a strong Prime Minister who would break but not bend. Thus, the political events gave rise to strong Prime Ministership and a Prime Ministerial system grew in course of time.

Due to sudden and violent death of Indira Gandhi, her son Rajiv Gandhi was inducted in as Prime Minister and again the Congress

Party obtained a huge majority with a young, handsome popular and energetic leader as the Prime Minister. It was after his Ministry's performance was seen by the people that the whole political picture changed in 1989 general elections. Probably, for the first time in Indian Parliamentary history a 'hung parliament' came into existence, without any party enjoying absolute majority. V.P Singh formed a lame ministry with support from out side (of the B.J.P.) and Rajiv Gandhi as leader of opposition. It was here that the system again reverted to a parliamentary system from an hitherto Prime Ministerial system. Even after the tragic assassination of Rajiv Gandhi, in spite of the so-called 'sympathy wave' the Congress did not get absolute majority in the May 1991 elections and the Tenth Lok Sabha again became a hung parliament with lame Ministry with support of some parties and groups given as a duty under duress or as some opposition leaders discribed it as a 'necessity of survival'(of the Government) and also because the Nation could not afford the luxury of polls at short intervals. As the polling figures indicate, the percentage of votes polled has also considerably dwindled pointing out to the fact that the people dislike frequent elections and are about to lose faith in leaders and the election process. Surprisingly enough the minority Ministry headed by P.V. Narasimaha Rao could usher economic changes, could survive Ayodhya debade and several bomb-blasts, could overcome Bank-scam and Harshad Mehta affair and Ramaswami impeachment episode, great scam events, which even a Ministry with majority of its own party could not have survived.

This brings us to another important point in constitutional theory. The parliamentary form of government presupposes the existence of a Two-party (Bi-party) system with one party getting absolute majority and the other sitting in opposition. In case the party in power is defeated, the opposition party with its leader steps in and shoulders the responsibility of government. Thus there is a reversal of roles but the government continues. This ideal situation obtains in Britain but does not exist in India. We have a multi-party system with about five to six all-India parties and other regional or localised parties or groups. Surprisingly enough, we could run the parliamentary system well right from 1950 to 1989 due to one monolithic party viz. the Congress with always a charismatic, monolithic leader in that party who used to be the Prime Minister and to enjoy national confidence. With the fall of the Congress party (its sub-division giving rise to small parties or groups with almost similar policy and programme but vying for political power) and subsequently the end of a charismatic leader acceptable to all factions within the party and by the nation as a whole, the unnatural scenario of a multi-party system delivering a stable parliamentary government come to an end. Now, unless there is a polarisation of parties on policy basis, reducing the system to a two or three-party system, or again a *charisma* dawns who will elevate one party to a superstructure, we are sure to get hung parliaments with on party getting an absolute majority to form a stable government on its own and has to take into confidence other parties and groups within the parliament for its survival. Ironically enough, the so-called hung parliament has brought into reality a 'parliamentary system' in which the parliament controls the ministry and not vice-versa i.e. the cabinet or the Prime Minister browbeating the parliament. However, as described in the preceding para, even a minority government could survive onslaughts on its credibility and performance because of a divided opposition, which can not join hands even to defeat a Ministry which they oppose.

Tottering of our Parliamentary Government

We adopted the British model of parliamentary form of government, alternatively called as 'Responsible Government' by political scientists. Inspite of a multi-party system it progressed well till Congress was in power at the centre as well as in States except isolated exceptions. As discussed earlier, Congress was a monolithic party with a monolithic leadership viz. that of the first Prime Minister Pt. Jawaharlal Nehru. Due to his charismatic leadership and personality, he did balance the left and the right wings in the party well. After his exit from the political scenario, the things went on changing fast. The multi-party system started showing its effects on politics and government. One-party could gain absolute majority and maintain stable government under Shri L.B. Shastri, Indira Gandhi and Rajiv Gandhi. But later, an era of instability started.

Between 1952 to 1996 total eleven elections were held for the Lok-Sabha; the first being of 1952 and the eleventh being in 1996. However the number of Governments i.e. of the Ministries amounts to seventeen. During 1952 to 1962 Pt. Nehru was the Prime Minister till he died in 1964. Between 1962 to 1967 there were three Ministries, viz. of Pt. Nehru, L.B. Shastri and Indira Gandhi. During 1967-71 there was only one Ministry but between 1967 to 1969 it was a Congress Ministry and from 1969 to 1971 it was a ministry supported by CPI from outside. During 1977 to 1985 there were three Ministries, out of which the first one under Morarji Desai was infact a conglomeration of five parties under one name. During 1980 upto the death of Indira Gandhi it was again a one-party majority government and this continued under Rajiv Gandhi with an unprecedented majority of one party in the Parliament.

Minority Governments

However the era of Minority governments is observed between 1989 to 1991first under V.P. Singh and later under Chandra Shekhar with support from outside. The Narasimha Rao ministry which came in power in 1991 was a minority government of Congress party and it survived a no-confidence motion in the House due to defection of ZMM members, which of late, has become a national issue and is sub-judice. A typical characteristic of this Ministry was that it was a minority ministry when it came in power but became a majority backed ministry by the end of the term. In 1996, after the Lok Sabha election, BJP was the single largest party and no other party had absolute majority. The BJP formed a Ministry under Atal Bihari Vajpayee but could not get majority support on the floor of the House and hence the Prime Minister resigned without pressing for voting in the House. Then came the Deve Gowda Ministry formed by thirteen different splinter groups which had altogether different and even conflicting policies and programmes in their mainfestoes when they contested the elections. The largest constituent was the Janata Dal (45 members) and all taken together they formed a United Front of 177 members which was unconditionally supported by Congress from outside while BJP was the main opposition party. The party position in Lok Sabha as on the 11th April 1997, the day on which the Deve Gowda ministry was defeated on the floor of the House due to withdrawal of the support by Congress is given below.

Bhartiya Janata Party-alies	204
BJP	162
Shiv Sena	15
Bahujan Samaj Party	11
Shiromani Akali Dal	08
Samata Party	05
Haryana Vikas Party	03
United Front	177
Janata Dal	45
CPI-M	32
CPI	12
Tamil Manila Congress	20

Dravida Munetra Kazhagham	17
Samajwadai Party	17
Telugu Desam Party	17
RSP	05
Asom Gana Parishad	05
AIFB	03
Congress (T)	02
MGP	01
BKKP	01
Congress	140
Independents and Others	**21**
SJP (Rashtriya)	03
Muslim League	02
Kerala Congress (M)	01
MIM	01
ASDC	01
JMM	01
Sikkim Democratic Front	01
UGDP	01
Independents	08
Nominated	02
Vacancies	02
Total Excluding Speaker	***544***

Later, as per the suggestion of Congress Party the United Front elected another leader and formed Ministry with Indra Kumar Gujral. However the Tamil Manila Congress refused to join Ministry though assured support from outside. The Gujral Ministry obtained a vote of confidence in the House on 22-4-1997.

All these developments are indicative of the fact that due to the original multi-party system, the rise of regional parties which are supported regionally in states and due to groupism and split within national-level parties, the parliamentary form is facing a crisis. As has been observed in case of the Deve Gowda Ministry, there is lack of homogeneity, unity, and common thinking on policies and issues which are basic characteristics of a parliamentary form of government as envisaged in the British system. Even the criterion of one leader the Prime Minister of the Ministry is lost. Such a Ministry cannot remain responsbile to the Parliament (and even to the People) and answerability loses it significance. In fact these ministries are controlled by the parties supporting from outside and are rediculed as under

'Remote control'.

Hence, theoretically, it is essential to classify the parliamentary form of Government into two sub-types viz. the British form (under a Bi-party system) or a *Responsbile government* and the other one, an Indian form (under a Multi-party system) or a *Non-Responsible* government. In the other form, absence of answerability, loss of stability are unavoidable. When France was facing similar situation De Gaulles' Constitution (of the Fifth Republic) made necessary changes to eliminate these defects and made the President powerful though not like that of the American President, thus bringing stability to the Government. It is high time that we as a nation re-think on the role of the President (Rashtrapati) in such a political situation and make necessary changes in the Constitution if required.

REFERENCE

1. Pylee, M.V., *Constitutional Government in India,* Asia Publishing House, Bombay, 1965, p. 369.

2

THE PARLIAMENT

India has a bi-cameral parliament called Sansad. The lower House is the House of the People or Lok Sabha and the upper House is the Council of States or Rajya Sabha. While the lower House represents—as the name suggests—the People of India, the *Rajya Sabha* is a federal House representing the States in the Indian Union. Consequently, an Indian citizen can contest for the Lok Sabha from any Lok Sabha constituency in India, for contesting seat for Rajya Sabha he ought to have domicile in the state from where he wants the contest for representation.

Lok Sabha—(House of the People)

Lok Sabha is elected for a term of five years. People send their representative from single member constituencies, by direct election, and through secret ballot. Any citizen who has completed 25 years of age and is not disqualified may contest the election. All citizens who have completed 18 years of age can vote. The maximum number of Membership of Lok Sabha is 552* and two Anglo-Indians may be nominated by the President if not already returned through elections. Seats are allotted to each state in proportion to the population. But of late the delimitation of constituencies has been made on the basis of the 1971 census figures and upto year 2001 there will be no reallocation of seats. Universal adult (at the completion of 18 years of age) franchise forms the basis of elections thought territorial constituencies within states. In all, 530 representatives are elected from the states and 20 from Union Territories. At present the total membership of the House

* Raised to 552 (not more than 530 representatives from the States, not more than 20 from the Union Territories and two from Anglo-Indian community nominated by the President, if not elected as per Constitution (31st Amendment) Act of 1973 and Goa, Daman and Diu Reorganisation Act of 1987 w.e.f. 30-5-1987.

is 544. Though the duration of the Houses is of 5 years the President may dissolve it earlier. After the expiry of 5 years it automatically ceases to function. But during the period when emergency is proclaimed, Parliament by law may extend the life of Lok Sabha by one year at a time and this may continue repeatedly till emergency is withdrawn. When a defeated Ministry does not resign but the Prime Minister requests the President to dissolve the House, it is not incumbent on him to dissolve the House if he feels that other leader in the same House can form a Ministry. Hence the President may or may not accept his advice. When Morarji Desai Ministry resigned (1979), Charan Singh was asked to form Ministry, which he did, but could not face the House to seek vote of confidence and resigned. Later, Jagjivan Ram also staked a claim to form Ministry but the President felt it proper to seek a fresh mandate which he did and the party was defeated badly and other party (Congress-I) was returned to power. The only and the first instance of the Ministry being expressly defeated on the floor of the House by a no-confidence motion was that of the Chandra Shekhar Ministry (1991) after which the House was dissolved and fresh elections conducted. In April 1997, the United Front ministry headed by Deve Gowda was defeated on the floor of the House. A new U.F. Ministry with I.K. Gujral as Prime Minister was sworn in and won a confidence vote in Lok Sabha on 22 April, 1997.

In the election held in May-June 1991 we elected the Tenth Lok Sabha in which no single political party got absolute mojority for forming a ministry on its own strength. This was repeated in 1996 when thirteen parties joined to for a United Front government.

Rajya Sabha (Council of States)

This Second Chamber (or Upper House) represents the States in our federation. However, unlike the United States of America we have given unequal representation to states depending upon their population. During the Constituent Assembly debates when many members raised the point of equal representation to states like that in the U.S.A., Nehru maintained that democratic basis of representation was the best according to which all states are given representation as per their population. Now that even in the United States, there is demand for amending the Constitution for giving representation to States on population basis (because due to the equal representation, numerically more states with less than the total population of U.S., get an edge over a few states with more than half of the U.S. population) in their Senate, we feel that ours was a correct view.

The minimum age for contesting for the Membership of Rajya Sabha is 30 years. The maximum number of elected representatives is 238. The election is held indirectly, as the Members of State Assemblies (Vidhan Sabhas) elect the members to this House, in accordance with the method of proportional representation by means of a single transferable vote. This is how states are represented in the Rajya Sabha. Rajya Sabha is a continuing body and is never dissolved. One-third of its Members retire after every two years and new members are returned. Thus the total term of a Member is of six years. At present the total number of elected Members is 233. The President nominates twelve members to this House from amongst those who have special knowledge or practical experiences of such matters as literature, art, science and social service. They too are appointed in rotation after an interval of two years.

The Vice-President of India is the ex-officio Chairman of the Rajya Sabha.

Speaker

After fresh elections of Lok Sabha are held and the new House reassembles, the first thing to do is to elect a Speaker, an office which is created much on the lines of the Speaker of the House of Commons in Great Britain. Though it is much similar certain conventions that grew in Britain could not be cultivated in India. The Speaker in India could not be above politics in the sense it is in Britain. Though Speakers in India have given a high prestige to the office and conducted the business in an objective, non-partisan manner, the position, 'once a speaker, always a speaker' could not be brought into practice. Here he is a party nominee and supported by majority party. At the constituency level, even well-known Speakers could not get elected unopposed firstly because the persons are not so exclusively above party-politics and secondly because the number of independent candidates is much more here (unlike in Britain) and they are not under any party's control, for being persuaded not to contest. Once contest takes place, party backing and involvement becomes essential. The first Speaker of Lok Sabha Shri P.G. Mavlankar established many new traditions adding to the position, prestige, and authority of the speaker. He discarded the use of the woollen wig to be put on head by Speakers (a British practice) stating that it was unsuitable for Indian climate.

The Speaker presides over and conducts the proceedings of the House as per rules and gives rulings on points of order and procedure.

He is responsible for the orderly conduct of proceedings and maintains discipline and order in the House. He can warn Members, reprimand or ask a Member to go out of the House. He may suspend a Member for a few days or for session. His decision on whether a Bill is money-bill or not is final. He dose not participate in discussions and does not vote except when he casts a casting-vote in case of a tie. It is through him that privileges of the House and of the Members are safeguarded. He administers the punishment for contempt of the House or breach of privileges. Conduct of debate, and giving opportunity to Members to speak is his job and he can apportion time for Members as well as for discussion on particular points. His decisions cannot be challenged in any Court of law. In his absence the Deputy Speaker performs his functions. Their salaries, fixed by Parliament by law, form a non-votable item and are charged on the Consolidated Fund of India. Like Britain there is no *Mace* on the Table of the Speaker and one of the reasons is that it is not necessary, as we don't have a Committee of the Whole House.

So far as the conduct of the business of both the Houses is concerned the following officers are important:

Lok Sabha: (i) Speaker
(ii) Deputy Speaker
(iii) Secretary General

Rajya Sabha: (i) Chairman
(ii) Deputy Chairman
(iii) Secretary-General

Their role and functions in some detail are given below keeping in view the actual parliamentary practice in India.

Officers of the Lok Sabha

The Speaker of Lok Sabha (Lok Sabha Adhyaksha)

The Speaker is chosen by the Lok Sabha from among its Members. He holds office until he ceases to be a member of the House or until he himself resigns his office or is removed from his office by Resolution of the House passed by a majority of all the Members of the House. He continues in office even after the House is dissolved and vacates it immediately before the first meeting of the new House. The Speaker is a symbol of impartiality. He disassociates himself from the party to which he belongs. He cannot vote except in the event of equality of votes (Casting-vote).

The Speaker exercises his duties partly under the Constitution and partly under the Rules Procedure and Conduct of Business in Lok Sabha. He is the principal spokesman of the House and represents its collective voice. His main duties are as under :

(1) to authenticate that a bill has been passed by the House before it is presented to the President for assent;
(2) to certify a Bill as a Money Bill;
(3) to preside over the joint sitting called to resolve disagreement between the two Houses of Parliament over a legislative measure;
(4) to admit notices of questions, resolutions and motions;
(5) to fix the time of the commencement and termination of a sitting and determine the days on which the House will sit;
(6) to regulate the proceedings in the House and maintain dignity and decorum. For this purpose he calls the members of the House to speak, proposes and puts the necessary questions and announces the decision of the House. He checks the relevancy of debates, stops unnecessary repetitions and accepts the closure of debates;
(7) to protect the rights and privileges of the House, its committees and all its Members irrespective of the party to which they may belong;
(8) to provide reasonable opportunity to all parties and groups to express their views on matters under consideration in the House;
(9) to ensure security arrangements in the Parliament House and its Annexe;
(10) to regulate admission of visitors and Press Correspondents to the galleries and other precincts of the Parliament House;
(11) to interpret the Constitution relating to parliamentary matters and the Rules of Procedure. His decision is final;
(12) to order expunction of passages from the records and once he does that, no one can publish them;
(13) to check disorderly behaviour in the House by asking the Member concerned to withdraw from the House for a day or part of a day for disorderly behaviour or even to suspend a Member from the services of the House on a proper motion moved for gross disorderly behaviour.
(14) to determine whether a *prima-facie* case exists for a matter

relating to a breach of privilege or contempt of the House or the conduct of a member being raised or referred to a committee for investigation, and if he withholds his consent the matter does not proceed further; and

(15) to appoint Chairmen of Parliamentary Committees and to issue them directions in all matters relating to their working and the procedure to be followed by them. The 52nd Amendment of 1985, which introduced the Tenth Schedule—the Anti-Defection law—has made the Speaker the sole and final arbiter regarding the question of disqualification of Members without provision of appeal to an outside authority.

Deputy Speaker of Lok-Sabha (Upadhyaksha of Lok Sabha)

Like the Speaker, the Deputy Speaker is elected by the House of the People from amongst its members. He holds office until he ceases to be a member of the House, or until he himself resigns his office, or is removed by a resolution of the House passed by a majority of the members of the House. Whenever the Speaker is absent, the Deputy Speaker presides over the deliberations of the House and for the time being excises all the powers of the Speaker under the rules of Procedure. Whenever he is nominated or appointed a member of a Committee, he is automatically Chairman of the Committee. Even otherwise he has a right to be present at any Committee and may, for the time being, preside over its deliberations though in practice he dose not attend committees on which he has not specifically been nominated. His duties are as onerous as those of the Speaker, for he presides over the House for the greater part of a sitting, while the Speaker is busy in attending to other parliamentary matters in his Chamber. The Deputy Speaker's rulings are final in so far as the matters under discussion on which they were given are concerned, but the Speaker may for the sake of certainty of procedure and uniformity of practice give general guidance to be followed in future in similar circumstances. Occasionally the Deputy Speaker may reserve a matter for ruling by the Speaker or may consult him before giving decision. Unlike the Speaker, the Deputy Speaker has however a right to speak in the House to take part in its deliberations and to vote on any proposition before the House as a member, but this he can do only when the Speaker is presiding. When himself in the Chair, the Deputy Speaker cannot vote except in the event equality of votes cast on any matter before the House.

When the Speaker is absent from a joint sitting of the Houses of

Parliament, the Deputy Speaker presides and exercises the powers of the Speaker at such a sitting as is the case when he is presiding over the deliberation of the House.

If both the Speaker and the Deputy Speaker are absent from sitting one of the members of the House out of panel of six Chairmen, whom the Speaker, nominates from time to time, presides. Like the Deputy Speaker, the Chairman has all the powers of the Speaker for the time he is presiding. A Chairman can give a ruling which is binding in the case or the point or proposition that he decides and he exercises all other powers in the same way as the Speaker. A Chairman, however, frequently reserves major issues for decision by the Speaker so that there is an authoritative ruling.

Secretary-General, Lok Sabha

The third important officer of the House is the Secretary-General. He is the adviser to the Speaker and to the House through the Speaker. He discharges on behalf of the Speaker all administrative and excutive functions and renders services and provides facilities to the members. He is the keeper of all parliamentary records. He is the head of the Secretariat of the House and is responsible for its administration, for maintaining discipline and for seeing that the secretarial work of the House and its committees is organised properly and conducted efficiently and smoothly. He provides secretarial assistance and staff to all the Parliamentary Committees and is available to them for advice. His role is that of a friend, philospher and guide to the members and the Committees.

Apart from his administrative and executive duties, the Secretary-General issues summons on behalf of the President asking members to attend a session of the House. He authenticates Bills in the absence of the Speaker, sends and receives messages on behalf of the House, receives notices, petitions, documents and papers addressed to or intended for the House, issues summons under his signature to witnesses to appear before the House or committees thereof, corresponds with members and others on behalf of the Speaker, issues admission tickets to the galleries, controls the finances and accounts of the House and its secretariat, circulates lists of business; bulletins and notices of amendments, prepares the journal, minutes and verbatim records of the House, arranges for the supply of the information to members on the various subjects in which they are interested, organises delegations abroad and attends to numerous other activities of Parliament in so far as its secretarial side is concerned. He is also responsibile for preparing and organising the secretarial duties of the Conference of Presiding Officers of Legislative Bodies in India, Conferences of Chairmen of various Legislatures and Parliamentary Committees in India, and for arranging extra-parliamentary activities such as addresses by distinguished persons to members, receptions, the sending of Parliamentary good-will missions abroad or receiving such missions from foreign countries.

Officers of the Rajya-Sabha

The Chairman of Rajya-Sabha

The Vice-President of India is *ex-officio* Chairman of the Council of States; but during any period when the Vice-President acts as President or discharges the functions of the President he does not perform the duties of the office of the Chairman of the Council of States. The Vice-President is elected by the members of both the Houses of Parliament assembled at a joint meeting in accordance with the system of proportional representation by means of single transferable vote and the voting at such elections is by secret ballot. The Vice-President is not a member of either House of Parliament or of a House of legislature of any state. The Vice-President holds office for a term of five years from the date on which he enters upon his office or until he resigns his office or is removed from his office by a resolution of the Council of states passed by a majority of the members of the Council and agreed to by the House of the People. The functions and duties of the Chairman of the Council of States are the same as those of the Speaker of the House of the People which have been described above.

Deputy Chairman, Rajya Sabha

The Deupty Chairman of the Council of States is elected from amongst its members. He holds office until he ceases to be a member of the Council or he resigns his office or is removed from the office by the Council by a majority of its members. The Deputy Chairman as Presiding Officer of the Council of States, exercises in all respects the same duties, functions and powers as the Deputy Speaker of the House of the People. The Chairman of the Council of States nominates a panel of members called Vice-Chariman one of whom presides whenever the Chairman and the Deputy Chairman are absent from the sitting of the Council.

Secretary General, Rajya Sabha

The Secretary General of the Council performs the same functions and duties in relation to the Council of States as the Chairman and the Secretary-General of the House of the people.

The High Traditions and Culture

Officers and staff of the Sectariats of the two Houses of parliament have built up high traditions of service of the Country, its people and Parliament. When a person is selelcted to enter upon his career as a Parliament official, every effort is made to inculcate in him the qualities expected of a Parliamentary official. An Ideal Parliamentary official should have the following qualities:

(i) He should have an objective approach and hold a balance between opposing view-points. This is necessary because unlike a civil servant, a Parliamentary official has to serve simultaneously both the Government of the day as also those who are opposed to it.

(ii) He should imbibe in him a spirit of tolerance and impartiality.

(iii) His job is to supply whatever factual information is desired by his officers or Members inrrespective of what his personal views are.

(iv) He should have enormous fund of patience and self-control in dealing with Members. A person who gets provoked easily is not fit to be a successful Parliamentary official. One must have a pleasant personality, adjustable nature and amiable manners.

(v) He should have a conviction that by pursuing a career of a Parliamentary official, he is serving Parliament and through it the people of India.

(vi) When a work assigned to him is accomplished, he should not brag about it or seek cheap pubiicity.

(vii) If he happens to be serving a Parliamentary Committee, he should ensure that Minutes of the sittings of the committee and its Reports are couched in a language which is dignified, courteous and of a standard expected of a Parliamentary Committee.

(viii) He should go on increasing the frontiers of his knowledge, develop the habit of reading newspapers, journals, magazines, reports and books to update his knowledge and keep himself abreast of developments not only in his country but also in other countries of the World.

(ix) He should understand that nature of work hardly matters and that what matters is, how it is done. Excellence should be the motto. Parliamentary work brooks no delay. He should, therefore, ensure that all work is disposed of in time.

The Powers of Parliament

The scope of powers of the Parliament is extremely vast. The Council of Ministers is the grand executive committee of Parliament charged with the responsibility of governing the country for and on behalf of the Parliament. It is virtually a circle within the broader circle of Parliament. Its members must be Members of Parliament and it continues to function only so long as it enjoys the confidence of the Parliament. Parliament exercises political as well as financial control over the Council of Ministers. The executive is accountable and answerable to the Parliament for its financial as well as administrative actions and omissions. Through its Committees, it inspects the important actions and censures the Ministry or a particular Minister for lapses and misdeeds. Through budget and fiscal policy, it can control the administration effectively. Through Impeachment of the President it controls the nominal head, while expressing lack of confidance is the patent way of controlling the real executive i.e. the Council of Ministers. Of-course so far as answerability of the Ministry and financial powers are concerned, it is the Lok-Sabha which enjoys the real power, while the Rajya-Sabha has nominal powers. Money-bills are first introduced in Lok-Sabha and can be delayed only for 14 days after which they are sent for Presidents' consent presuming as if they are okayed by Rajya-Sabha. If only Lok-Sabha passes a vote of no-confidence, the Ministry has to resign but if only Rajya-Sabha passes such a motion the Ministry need not resign.

Parliament has wide powers to pass laws on subjects from the Union List (97) and its laws get precedence over State laws (in case of disagreement) so far as laws on subjects from Concurrent List (47) are concerned. Even for the State List (66) the Parliament may pass a law with prior consent from Rajya-Sabha which can be given for one year at a time. During emergency proclamation in a State, President can empower parliament to pass laws for the state. The Residuary powers are also with the Parliament.

It is only the Parliament which can initiate a constitutional amendment and for most of the parts (excepting Articles 54, 55, 73, 162, 241, Chapter IV of Part V, Chapter V of Part VI, Chapter I of

Part XI, lists in Seventh Schedule, representation of States in Parliament, and Article 368—Amendment procedure), all other parts/articles can be amended by Parliament without concurrence of the State legislatures. All ordinances promulgated by President must receive Parliament's approval failing which they cease to operate.

The Parliament can recommed removal of Supreme Court and High Court judges by special majority on the basis of which President can remove the judge.

In case of differences over an ordinary bill a joint sitting of both the Houses of Parliament may be called, over which Speaker of Lok Sabha presides. The fate of the Bill is decided by simple vote in the joint sitting but considering that Lok-Sabha membership is almost more than double than that of the Rajya Sabha, the verdict goes mostly on the side of Lok Sabha.

Political Parties and Parliament

A Parliamentary system pre-supposes a bi-party system. In India we have had a multi-party system due to which many parties (at least 5-6 at the All India level) and a few regional parties are representing people in Lok-Sabha. Defections from parties galored, destabilising ministries in States and at the Center.

Party Position In Lok Sabha
(As on 22-02-1992, after Punjab Polls)

Party	Seats
Congress (I)	243
BJP	119
Janata Dal	58
CPI (M)	35
CPI	14
TDP	13
AIDMK	11
JMM	5
SJP	5
RSP	4
Shiva Sena	4
AIFB	3
Muslim League	2
Congress - S	1
AIMEM	1
ASDC	1

AGP	1
JD(G)	1
HVP	1
K C (MANI)	1
MPP	1
NPC	1
SSP	1
IND	1
Unattached	1
NOM	2
Vacancies	11
Total (Excluding Speaker)	544

The Anti-Defection Amendment

The Constitution (Fifty-Second Amendment) Act, passed in 1985, is designed to prevent the scourge of defection of members of Parliament and state legislatures from one political party to another, and destabilizing governments in the process.

(1) A member of a House belonging to any political party becomes disqualified for being a member of the House—

(a) If he voluntarily given up his membership of such political party; or

(b) if he votes or abstains from voting in such House contrary to any direction issued by the political party to which he belongs without obtaining prior permission of such party, and such act has not been condoned by the concerned political party within 15 days from the date of such voting.

An elected member of a House belongs to the political party by which he was set up as a candidate for election. An independent member of a House (elected without being set up as a candidate by any political party) shall become disqualified to remain a member of the House if he joins any political party.

The disqualification on the ground of defection does not apply when there is a split in the concerned political party and he belongs to a faction arising out of such split and such group consists of not less than 1/3 members of the party. Similarly, no disqualification arises when his party merges with another political party.

Any question regarding disqualification arising out of defection is to be decided by the Chairman of Rajya Sabha or the Speaker of the House as the case may be, and his decision shall be final. The Courts do not have any jurisdiction in such a matter.

This is a strange amendment in so far as it refers to and purports to amend something which does not find place in the original constitution viz. 'political party'. In fact, except erstwhile Soviet Union's Constitution in which there was a reference to political party (The Communist Party) and that of the Communist Republic of China no democratic constitution has had such a mention. It was a phenomenon having *de facto* existance in politics but not a *de jure* one. Though a situation had been created due to political defections which warranted some check, this amendment has put political party above peoples' representation thus sub-ordinating electorate's interest to that is political parties. When Winston Churchill, the then British Prime-Minister, was asked the priorities of his allegiance he had said, "Nation first, electorate next, and party last." Had Churchill been under the above provisions he could have been disqualified from Membership. If a Member honestly feels that taking a particular stand on a particular issue is right, and that he also gets a mandate from his electorate accordingly, but, if the party on whose banner he was elected takes a different stand, either he has to keep his conscience in cold storage and displease his electors or to get disqualified "for voting or abstaining from voting . . . . contrary to the direction issued by his political party". Specially on issues relating to public interest, health, etc. e.g. a policy on prohibition, if a Member takes a stand which may be in tune with the Directive Principles but his party takes a different stand, he will be compelled to vote with his party, against his conscience. Similarly, the main object behind this was to check destabilizing of the governments, but from the 1989 and 1991 election results it has been observed that no political party will now get an absolute majority to form stable government on its own and will have to depend upon different party groups for survival. This again brings back to a position which the above amendment purported to avoid. The net result is, that the *raison d'tre* of becoming a people's representative has been knocked down without ultimately bringing stability.

Of late, the quality of the parliamentary discussions, debates and demenour has largely suffered, there is a subsequent deterioration in the political executives and their sensitivity towards parliamentary responsibility and a consequent strengthening of bureaucracy almost to the extent of riding over democracy.

Controversies on the Anti-Defection Amendment

As discussed earlier it was obvious that some serious review was necessary of some provisions. In the initial enthusiasm it was not viewed in the right perspective. Defections still continued. The flaw came to the fore when some members of the Shiv Sena defected to Congress-I in the Maharashtra Legislative Assembly (Winter Session of 1991 at Nagpur). The Speaker okayed the continuing of membership of those Members and Shiv Sena had no legal recourse to oppose the dicision.

In February 1992, Brij Mohan Mishra Speaker of Madhya-Pradesh Vidhan Sabha was critical of a recent Supreme Court decision in the superme court struck down para 7 of the Tenth Schedule* and made Speaker's decision amenable to judicial review; calling it as an 'interference of courts' under the 'garb of judicial review'.

The events during the last few years indicated that shrewd politicians had found a way to use the provision to their advantage, against the spirit of law. In India we could not develop the image of a Speaker who is always above party politics (which could have led to a situation of 'once a Speaker, always a Speaker'. On the contrary unhealthy practices like appointing ex-Speakers to Ministers' posts, or Speakers participating, directly or indirectly in the activities of Pressure groups have been adopted. It is in this context that the move to have a system of judicial review was also welcomed by many people.

A conference of Speakers convened under the able Chairmanship of Shivaraj Patil, Speaker, Lok Sabha in February 1992 suggested a system of review by an independent authority either by a body of Speakers or by President or Governors. Such a review of a Speaker's decision under Anti-Defection law may be opposed by politicians. Similarly, review of such a vital decision by head of the executive (President/Governor) may also not be acceptable as these 'nominal' heads under our parliamentary system are likely to be 'advised' by their ministries which will always be branded as 'partisan'. Hence a body of Speakers or some such mechanism which will establish its credibility may be more acceptable. The problem remains whether such functions being exercised under our Constitution could totally be removed from judicial review.

---

* Kihoto Hollohan V. Zachillhu & Others, S.C. Judgment delivered in Feb. 1992.

The object of the tenth Schedule is to curb the evil of political defections motived by lure of office or other similar considerations which endanger the foundations of our democracy. The remedy proposed is to disqualify the Member who has defected, from continuing as a Member of the House. It distinguishes between cases of 'split' in the original party or merger of parties from that of defection. The authority to decide the dispute about disqualifying a Member vests in the Chairman or the Speaker of the House, and his decision is final. A five-judge bench of the Supreme Court in its decision in *Shri Kihoto Hollohan* v. *Shri Zachillhu and others* (Feb. 1992) upheld the validity of Anti-defection law, but made it subject to the Judicial review. These Judges termed the provisions of anti-defection law as salutory, intended to strengthen the fabric of Indian Parliamentary democracy by curbing unprincipled and unethical political defections.

The minority view expressed by two Judges termed the whole of this constitutional amemdment defective for absence of ratification as required under the proviso to Article 368 (2). It was felt that the authority to decide the question of disqualification of a member of Legislative is outside the jurisdiction of the House, as envisaged by Articles 103 and 192. In contrast to this, the Tenth Schedule makes the Speaker not only the sole arbiter but the final authority in such dispute without provision of appeal against his decision. Finding fault with this adjudicatory function, as being inconsistent with the constitutional scheme, the minority opinion considered it as a breach of basic feature of constitution, and hence was of the view that the entire Tenth Schedule must be struck down as unconstitutional.

The whole issue attracted the attention of the nation due to the ruling given by the Lok Sabha Speaker on the split in the Janata Dal caused by the break away Ajit Singh faction. The Speaker's ruling that 16 of the original group of 20 MPs did not come under the anti-defection rule, but 4 of them would incur the wrath of the Tenth Schedule was not understood, as common people could not grasp the difference in the nature of the action of 16 MPs and that of the disqualified 4 MPs. The basic question was whether allotment of different seats would amount to defection and also whether the conduct inside the House and that outside the House should be separated.

It is difficult for the Speaker to monitor and know the factual position of the happenings inside the political party (but outside the House) and he has to depend upon the verdict of the leader from the concerned party. Hence, some experts have opined that the ultimate decision on the issue of defection should rest on the individual legislator's admission about his quitting the party and not on anything else, not even his refusal. To obey his party's whip. To add a new dimension to the whole issue, the survival of Narasimha Rao government in the voting on no-confidence motion in the Lok Sabha (Aug. 1993) with the help of 7 'defector' Members of Janata Dal (Ajit Singh faction) has put into sharp focus the Tenth Schedule and given rise to the doubts on its utility and ethical context. The case of bribery of the four Zarkhand Mukti Morcha M.Ps (which is in the court) in which the Rao Government survived on their defection secured allegedly by giving bribe is a slap on the face of the amendment. It sounds as if the democratic rights and privileges have been subjugated to the political exigencies and conveniences of our parliamentary system. Hence it is necessary to review the propriety of the Tenth Schedule and it may be advisable to adopt the procedure of 'recall' in all such cases of defection thus making the electorate the sole and final arbiter of the case.

Parliamentary Control Over the Executive

Parliamentary control over the executive is exercised by controlling the Ministry. In fact the real control is by the House of the People i.e. the Lok Sabha and not the Rajya Sabha as the Ministry has to resign only if it loses the confidence of the Lok Sabha. Usually the following occasions are considered as indicative of loss of confidence:

(i) The President delivers the inaugural address at the opening of the first session of the Parliament every year. His speech is drafted by the Prime-Minister and contains references to the performance of the Ministry in the previous years and its future policy and programmes. If the vote of thanks on the President's, address is not carried, it amounts to a loss of confidence and the Ministry must resign.
(ii) If a Money-Bill is lost on cuts suggested by Private Members in the Budget are approved by the House, it amounts to no-confidence.
(iii) If an ordinary bill which is prestigious for the Government is lost or a Private Members Bill strongly opposed by the Government is carried, it is loss of confidence.
(iv) If a Censure Motion against a Minister or his Ministry is passed, unless the Ministry lets him down, it amounts to no-confidence against the whole Ministry due to collective responsibility.
(v) A no-confidence motion which is against the whole Ministry

and may be in simple language, offers a wide scope to discuss any subject pertaining to any or all Ministries. If this is passed, the Ministry has to resign.

Usually, the Prime-Minister intervenes in all discussions about confidence in the Ministry.

If a no-confidence motion is passed either the Prime-Minister tenders his resignation to the President which means the dissolution of the whole Ministry or else he may advise the president to dissolve the Lok Sabha and order fresh elections. The stand behind such advice is that the electorate is behind his ministry, though the elected representatives have gone against them. It purely in the Presidents' discretion to accept that advice or not. If he feels that others can form a stable government he may give an opportunity to other leader of the House by appointing him as a new Prime-Ministers. However, if he feels that none can form a stable government the best alternative is to seek the verdict of the electorate by dissolving the Lok Sabha and ordering new elections of the House. After Shri Morarji Desai's exit the then President N. Sanjeeva Reddy appointed Shri Charan Singh as Prime Minister but after he did not face the House and prove his majority, the President ordered dissolution of the House and ordered fresh elections. The out-come of the elections showed that his decision was correct as the caretaker ruling party lost and other Party obtained peoples mandate.

A Minister is responsible to the House and when the House expresses no-confidence the Minister has to resign. In this case the displeasure incurred is that of the House. But when a Minister is guilty of corruption of bribery or some such act which is his personal mistake the President can dismiss him (of course on the advice of the Prime Minister) which then will be Presidents' displeasure in a true-sense. One must remember that due to political patronage even a Minister's mistake may be backed by a ministry and by the Prime Minister making it a prestige issue and the whole Ministry may stake its prospects and they may then stand together or fall together, while in case of a less favourite Minister he may be made a scape goat and left to the high seas—to be swallowed by the political crocodiles.

In Great Britain, the exact position of the Prime Minister is traditionally described as 'first among equals (primus inter pares)', i.e. he is a leader of the team and not a chief, much less a boss. This is because the post is a product of historical growth, born out of conventions and convenience and not a part of written words.

This position was also recongised by the Supreme Court and

stated clearly while delivering judgment in Rai Saheb Ram Jawaya Kanpur and others v. The State of Punjab. (1995, S.C. 25—C.R. 225, pp. 236-237) and V.N. Rao v. Indira Gandhi (1971), 2 S.C.C. 63) the Court observed, 'the President has been made a formal or constitutional head of the executive and the real executive powers are vested in the Minister or the Cabinet'. It further commented, 'In the Indian Constitution we have the same system of Parliamentary executive as in England and the Council of Ministers consisting, as it does, of the Members of Legislature is, like the British Cabinet, a hyphen which joins, a buckle which fastens the legislative part of the state to the executive part. The Cabinet enjoying a majority in the legislature concentrates in itself the virtual control of both, legislative and executive functions; and as the Ministers constituting the Cabinet have presumably agreed on fundamentals and act on the principle of collective responsibility, the most, important questions of policy are formulated by them.'

Thus, in India there is a direct and continuous responsibility of the Ministry to the Parliament, and the Prime Minister occupies a position similar to that in Great Britain—'The key-stone of the Cabinet arch'. A Minister must be a member of either of the Houses or get membership within six months or else he has to quit the Ministry. He is also responsible for every decision of the Council and if he disagrees, he must resign and come out of it.

Responsibility to the Parliament

Article 53 of the Constitution Provides that the executive power of the Union is vested in the President and it is to be exercised by him either directly or through officers subordinate to him, in accordance with the Constitution. Article 74 provides that there shall be a Council of Ministers, with the Prime Minister at the head to aid and advise the President who shall in the exercise of his functions act in accordance with such advice. (Article 74 (i)). Though he may require the Council of Ministers to reconsider such advice either generally or otherwise, the President shall act in accordance with the advice tendered after reconsideration, Article 75 (3) provides that the Council of Ministers is to be collectively responsible to the House of the People. The Constitution also states that the Ministers hold office during 'the pleasure of the President'. However, while replying to the doubts raised by Dr. Rajendra Prasad, who was the Chairman of the Constituent Assembly, Dr. Ambedkar had explained that though the 'pleasure' is of the President, it will be decided by the House of the

People,* i.e. when he loses confidence of the House or when the President is convinced that Minister's administration is not pure.

The President and the Parliament

President's Address

The President may address both Houses of Parliament assembled together or either House of Parliament separately in the following three cases :

The Annual Address

Under Article 87 (1) of the Constitution, at the commencement of the first session after the general election to Lok Sabha and at the commencement of the first session of each year the President is required to address both Houses of Parliament assembled together and inform Parliament of the causes of its summons. This address has to be to both Houses of Parliament assembled together which means that if at the time of commencement of the first session of the year of Rajya Sabha, Lok Sabha has been dissolved, then Rajya Sabha can have its session without the President's address. This happened in 1977 when during dissolution of Lok Sabha, Rajya Sabha had its session on the 1st February 1977 without President's Address.

A Special Address

Under Article 86 (1) of the Constitution the President may address either House of Parliament or both Houses assembled together and for that purpose require the attendance of members. There has been no such special address so far.

Address at the time of Prorogation

Under Rule 24 of the Rules of Procedure and Conduct of business in Lok Sabha, when the President prorogues the House or Houses, he may address the House or Houses, as the case may be. There has been no such address so far.

---

* Constituent Assembly Debates-VII, p. 1158.

President's Address or 'Abhibhashan'

The President's Address at the commencement of the first session of the year is a regular feature. This Address which may be called *Abhibhashan,* is a statement of policy of the Government and it is not the President but the Government who are responsible for the contents of the 'Address'. It contains a review of various activities and achievements in different spheres including international field during the previous year and the policy of the Government with regard to important internal and international problems. It also indicates the main items of legislative business which are proposed to be brought before Parliament during the sessions to be held in that year.

The President addresses both Houses of Parliament assembled together after the members elected to Lok Sabha have made and subscribed the oath or affirmation and the Speaker has been elected. These preliminaries are usually completed in two days and the President's address is held the third day. In India, President's address is usually termed as *Abhibhashan* (A Sanskrit word). No other business is transacted till the President has addressed both Houses assembled together in the Central Hall. Half an hour after the President's address, both the Houses of Parliament meet separately in their own chambers. At the sittings of the two Houses so held, a copy of the President's Address is laid on the Table by the Secretary-General of the House to bring it on record of the House.

Some ceremonies are observed which make the President's Address a very solemn, dignified and colourful occassion. Members of both the Houses of Parliament assemble together in the Central hall of Parliament House at least five minutes the arrival of the President. In the Central Hall seats in the first few rows are reserved for Ministers, Deputy Speaker and Deputy Chairman of Rajya Sabha, leaders of parties, and groups in both Houses of Parliament. Remaining seats are occupied by members in any manner they like. Members are expected not to leave the Central Hall when President is addressing.

The President drives-in-states to Parliament House and arrives at the Parliament House in the State Coach driven by six horses, now (now in a bullet-proof car) attended by his Secretary and Military Secretary and escorted by his mounted bodyguards who wear colorful uniforms. When the President alights from the coach at gate No. 5 of Parliament House, his bodyguards give a 'National Salute'. Thereafter, the President is introduced to the Chairman of Rajya Sabha, Prime Minister, the Speaker of Lok Sabha, Minister of Parliamentary Affairs, Secretary-General of Lok Sabha and the Secretary-General of Rajya

Sabha. The President is conducted to the Central Hall in a procession. As soon as the procession enters the gangway of the Central Hall the Marshal of Lok Sabha announces, from the dais in Hindi: "Honourable Members, Honourable the President". Almost simultaneously, the two trumpeters positioned in the gallery facing the entrance to the Central Hall play the *bugles* and give a fanfare till the President reaches on the dais. On sounding the bugles members rise in their places remain standing until the Presidential procession reaches the dais and the President takes his seat. On reaching the floor of the Central hall in front of the dais, the procession bifurcates, the President, the Chairman of Rajya Sabha and the Speaker of Lok Sabha go to the dais and occupy their seats. Secretary-general of Lok Sabha, Military Secretary to the President and two ADCs, take their seats in the pit of the House to the left of the President and the Secretary-General of Rajya Sabha, Secretary to the President and two ADCs. take their seats in the pit of the House to the right of the President. The Prime Minister, the Minister of Parliamentary Affairs and other Ministers take the seats earmarked for them in the front row in the Central Hall. When the President reaches his seat at the dais, the band of Rashtrapati Bhavan, which is positioned in advance in one of the lobbies of Central Hall, plays the National Anthem. All visitors and members stand in their places when the National Anthem is played. Thereafter the President occupies his seat and delivers his address both in Hindi and English. After the President's address is over, the National Anthem is played once again. Thereafter, the President leaves the Central Hall in a procession which is formed on the same pattern as at the time of arrival of the President. Members remain standing till the President leaves the Central Hall. When the Presidential procession reaches the main gate of Parliament House, the Presiding Officers and Secretaries-General of the two Houses bid him farewell. Thereafter, the President's bodyguard again give him the 'National Salute'. Then the President gets into the coach and drives-in-state back to the Rashtrapati Bhawan.

The President's address to both Houses of Parliament assembled together is the most solemn and formal act under the Constitution. Utmost dignity and decorum befitting that occasion is maintained. The assembly of members of the two Houses to hear the President's address is not treated as sitting of either House. The President himself is the presiding officer at that time and he deals with any interruptions or disturbances at that time of the address. He can certainly take the assistances of Speaker, Lok Sabha of Chairman of Rajya Sabha in restoring order where necessary. However, any action on the part of the member which mars the occasion is taken seriously by the House to which the member belongs. That House may if it deems necessary, constitute a committee to go into the matter and on the recommendation of the committee, award suitable punishment to the member concerned. The House can itself also consider the matter and adopt a suitable motion disapproving the conduct of the member concerned.

The President's Address is discussed by each House of Parliament on a Motion of Thanks moved by a member and seconded by another member. Members who are to move and second the Motion are selected by the Prime Minister and Notice of such a Motion is received through the Minister of Parliamentary Affairs. The form of the motion is:

> "That the members of Lok Sabha assembled in this session are deeply grateful to the President for the Address which he has been pleased to deliver to both Houses of Parliament assembled together on . . . . .".

The discussion on Motion of Thanks lasts for 3 or 4 days. The scope of discussion on Parliament's Address is very wide and members are free to speak on all sorts of national or international problems. During the discussion a large number of amendments are moved by members highlighting certain issues which the President's Address failed to take note of or criticising the policy enunciated in the address or making suggestions for Government action. The discussion is initiated by the mover in whose name the Motion stands in the order paper. Then the seconder makes a speech seconding the Motion. After the seconder, other members speak. Time allotted by the House is distributed amongst various parties and groups proportionately to their respective strength. Members may be called alternately from the opposition and the ruling party to maintain balance and lively debate. At the end of the discussion, the Prime Minister replies to the debate. Thereafter, first the amendments are disposed of and then the Motion of Thanks is put to vote and adopted. After it is adopted, a communication is sent by the Speaker to the President conveying to him, the motion adopted by the House.

In reply to that communication, the President sends a message conveying his satisfaction on the Motion adopted by the House. The massage received from the President is reported to the House by the Speaker.

Adournment Motion

If it refers to some urgent, definite and recent matter of importance the Speaker may allow if it is in order and if 10 per cent (about 50) members support it.

An Adjournment motion seeks to adjourn the business as per the approved business for the day and to take-up some matter which is of public interest and is thus more urgent.

If an adjournment motion is admitted and after voting, is taken-up for discussion it amounts to a 'violent censure of the Government', however, the Government need not resign.

On this point an Hon'able Minister of State of Law and Justice opined that an adjournment is 'just a postponement of some item on the agenda and as such is not at all a censure of the Government'. However, one retired Chief Executive Officer of the Lok Sabha Secretariat who in August 1988 was in an Advisory Capacity to the Secretariat and the Deputy Director from Rajya Sabha Secretariat firmly held that if an adjournment motion is admitted after voting in the House, it amounts to a strong censure of the Government. It may be recalled here that since long even in Great Britain, resignation of a Ministry is not warranted if adjournment motion is admitted, though it is considered as a censure of the Government. An adjournment motion is supposed to draw the attention of the House to a recent matter of urgent public importance having serious consequences and in regard to which a motion or a resolution with proper notice will be too late. The matter proposed to be raised should be of such a character that something very grave which affects the whole country and its security has happened and the House is required to pay its attention immediately by interrupting the normal business of the House. The adjournment motion is thus an extraordinary procedure which, if admitted,leads to setting aside the normal business of the House for discussing a definite matter of urgent public importance. Such notices are treated as very important notices and considered very expeditiously and carefully. The motion can be moved with the consent of the Speaker only, and the refusal to give the consent is his absolute discretion and he is not bound to give any reason for the same.

The Procedure

Notice of an adjournment motion has to be given by the member in writing by 10.00 a.m. on the day on which the motion is to be moved. Notices received after 10.00 a.m. are deemed to be given for the next day.

Notice is addressed to Secretary-General and its copies are endorsed to the Speaker, the minister concerned and the Minister of

Parliamentary Affairs. All the copies of a notice are given by the member in the Parliamentary Notice Office. Copies of notices intended for Ministers have to be collected by the representatives of ministers themselves from Lok Sabha Secretariat (Table Office) between 10.30 hrs. and 11.00 hrs. and 16.00 hrs. Every Ministry is expected to send its representative between the aforesaid timings to find out whether any notice has been received for his Ministry and if so, to collect the copy from there and bring it to the notice of officers of the Ministry and the Minister immediately.

Adjournment motions are taken up in the House immediately after questions (including short Notice Questions). Whenever notices of an adjournment motion pertaining to a particular Ministry is tabled, the Minister concerned is expected to be ready with the facts and to be present in the House at the time adjournment motion is to be taken up. It is open to a Minister to bring immediately on receipt of notice of an adjournment motion any facts to the notice of the Speaker, which he may take into account in deciding the admissibility or otherwise of the notice. Where the notice is, according to Minister's information, based on an incorrect press report or lacks factual basis or attracts any other provision of the Rules of procedure to render it inadmissible, it is open to the Minister concerned to bring that fact to the notice of the Speaker. In many cases, notices of adjournment motions are disallowed by the speaker in his Chamber and the fact is communicated to the member through the lobby officer. This information is, however, not conveyed to the Minister, the reason being that even where notice of an adjournment motion has been disallowed by the Speaker and the member informed about it, it cannot be ruled out that the member might still try to raise the matter in the House. In such an eventuality if the Minister is available in the House to give the factual position about the matter sought to be raised and to point out as to how the notice is inadmissible under the rules, it helps the Speaker in checking the time of the House being taken up unnecessarily.

Procedure observed for the disposal of adjournment motions given below.

Where the Speaker is satisfied *prima facie* that the matter proposed to be discussed is in order under the rules, he gives his consent to the moving of the motion and at the appropriate time calls upon the member concerned to ask for leave to move the adjournment motion before the House. The Minister concerned may be informed about it where the time permits. If objection to leave being granted is taken, the Speaker requests those members who are in favour of leave being granted to rise in their places and if not less than 50 members rise accordingly, he declares that leave is granted. If, however, less than 50 members rise, the Speaker informs the member that he does not have the leave of the House.

If the leave of the house is granted, the motion 'that the house do now adjourn' is taken up at 15.00 hrs. or at an earlier hour if the speaker after considering the state of business in the House, so directs. The Speaker usually asks the Government to indicate the hour. The Speaker then takes the sense of the House and if the House agrees, the matter is taken up at that particular hour.

Where the Speaker is satisfied *prima facie*, that the notice of an adjournment motion is inadmissible, he refuses his consent without bringing the matter before the House and the member concerned is informed of the Speaker's decision

Once a member is informed of the Speaker's decision withholding his consent, no discussion or point is permitted to be raised in the House either on the subject matter of the notice or the reasons for disallowance thereof. If, however, the member wants to make a submission to the Speaker to reconsider his decision, he has to see the Speaker in his Chamber latter during the day or make a written representation to the Speaker.

The Speaker's decision either to bring the matter before the House or to withhold his consent outside, is final.

When giving his consent to an adjournment motion the Speaker is guided by the following principles:

(1) If the matter raised is *definite*. An adjournment motion is not admissible where the facts are not settled or unless it relates to some precise recent action or omission of the Government. Notices about threatened strike or likely dislocation of a service or about a situation which has not actually arisen are inadmissible.

(2) If the matter raised is *urgent*. A matter is deemed to be urgent only if it has arisen suddenly or is in the nature of an emergency. It should not be a continuing matter. The urgency should be such that the matter brooks no delay.

(3) When the matter raised is of *public importance*. The importance of the matter should warrant interruption of normal business of the House. It should be a larger issue than a merely individual grievance. It should be a question of public principle.

(4) It does not raise a question of privilege.

(5) It does not revive discussion on a matter already discussed in the same session.

(6) It does not anticipate a matter already discussed in the same session.

(7) It does not relate to matter which is sub-judice.

(8) It does not raise any question which under the Constitution or Rules can be raised on a distinct substantive motion.

(9) The matter involves direct or indirect responsibility of the Central Government.

Discussions on adjournment motion when admitted, usually commences at 4.00 p.m. and continues till 6.30 p.m. or beyoned that. The mover moves the motion "That the House do now adjourn". After the mover, other members speak. Then the Minister intervenes. At the end, the mover replies to the discussion. Thereafter, the Motion is put to vote. If the motion is negatived, the business which was interrupted by the adjournment motion is resumed or some other item is taken up before the House is adjourned for the day.

The purpose of an adjournment motion is to take the Government to task for a recent act of omission or commission having serious consequences. Adoption of an adjournment motion amounts to a sort of censure on Government.

Although no direct effect can be given to an adjournment motion, it is very likely that Government which has failed to prevent an adverse vote on an adjournment motion, will not be able to survive a direct motion of no-confidence on the Council of Minister.

Calling Attention Motions

A member may, with the previous permission of the Speaker, call the attention of a Minister to any matter of urgent public importance and request the Minister to make a statement on the subject. The Minister may either make a brief statement immediately or he may ask for time to make the statement at the later hour or date. There is no debate on such statement at the time it is made but each member in whose name the item stands in the list of Business may, with the permission of the Speaker, ask a specific and brief clarificatory question.

The main purpose of a calling attention is to seek an authentic statement from the concerned Minister on a matter of urgent public importance. This process does not involve any censure of the Government as there is no discussion or voting thereon.

Notices of calling Attention have to be given by members in writing by 10.00 a.m. Notices given after 10.00 a.m. are treated as notices received on the following day. Although there is no provision in the Rules for endorsing copies of notices of calling attention to the Minister concerned, under a convention which is now well established, each member deposits in the Notice office three copies of his notice, one for the Secretary-General to whom it has to be addressed, second for the Speaker, and third for the Minister concerned. Copies of the Notices intended for the Ministers are made available to representatives of the Ministries concerned from Table Office between 10.30 and 11.00 hrs. and between 16.00 and 16.30 hrs.

The following procedure is followed for dealing with Calling Attention Notices:

(1) All Calling Attention Notices received in a week are kept alive and placed before the Speaker from day-to-day along with the notices received upto 10 hrs. on the day on which the notices are put up to the Speaker who may select one of them for a statement by the concerned Minister at the next sitting of the House. On the last day of the week on which the House sits, the notices received upto 10.00 hrs. on that day are considered. Notices received after 10.00 hrs. on the last day of the week on which the House sits are deemed to have been received for the day on which the next sitting of the House is to be held and these are treated as valid for the following week.

    Name of only those members are balloted whose notices are received after 10.00 hrs. on the last day of the week on which the House sits and upto 10.00 hrs. on the day on which the notice is selected by the Speaker.

(2) If notices of more than one matter are received for the same day, the Speaker selects one matter which in his opinion is more urgent and important.

(3) The ballot of determining the relative priority of admitted calling attention notices on the same subject is held is the Lobby of the Central Hall, Parliament House.

(4) After the ballot, a copy of the entry to be made in the list of Business showing the names of five members who have secured priority in the ballot is put up on the Notice Boards for the information of Member.

(5) If a member has any objection to his name being added to the calling attention is the form in which it has been admitted by

the Speaker, he may inform the Chief Examiner of Bills and Resolutions, Lok Sabha Secretariat, immediately (but not later than the time the House rises for the day) in writing that his name may not be added to the Calling Attention in the List of Business.

(6) In certain cases, the Speaker may select two Calling Attention matters for one sitting. The second matter can be taken up at or immediately before the end of sitting as the Speaker may fix. However, the second matter cannot be raised by the same members who raise the first matter.

Where the Speaker desires to have a factual note on the subject or a note on the extent of responsibility of the Central Government, the notice is referred to the Minister concerned for a note. In such cases the notices are kept pending till a final decision is taken by the Speaker.

Where a calling attention notice is admitted by the Speaker, the members concerned are informed of the decision verbally. Simultaneously, the Minister is informed over the telephone about admission of the notice and the date on which the item is to be taken up.

Although under Rule 197, it is permissible for a Calling Attention Notice to be taken up on the same day on which the notice has been given. An entry about the notice admitted is invariably made in the printed list of Business of the day on which it is to be taken up. This procedure has an advantage in an much as it gives sufficient time to the Minister concerned to gather facts about the matter raised, to prepare a statement in time and to make copies thereof available for the use of the Speaker and members concerned.

Names of only 5 members are clubbed on a Calling Attention notice put down in the list of Business. These names are determined by ballot. As far as possible the text of the notice tabled by the member who has secured first placed in the ballot is followed for preparing the entry for the list of Business but the Speaker may make suitable amendments in the text given by the member in order to make it specific to the issue which has been selected and to remove any ambiguity. After the entry for the list of Business is settled, a copy thereof is sent to the Ministry concerned along with a note in continuation of telephonic intimation given earlier. This entry in the list of Business has to be the basis for Minister's statement but it is open to the Minister to cover various points raised in the notices on the subject, advance copies of which have already been collected by the Ministry.

When item regarding calling attention is reached in the House, the member whose name appears first in the list of Business calls the attention of the Minister and requests him to make a statement on the subject. In case the first member is absent, the attention is called by the second member and so on, but there is no procedure for authorisation of some other member to call the attention on behalf of a member. After attention is called, the Minister concerned makes statement on the subject. In case all the member in whose names the item stands in the list of business are absent the Minister can lay his statement on the Table of the House and the statement so laid will be treated as having been laid *suo moto.* If the minister does not lay the statement, the item lapses and it is not put down again.

It is now a settled practice that copies of the statement to be made by the Minister are made available to members, through Notice Office, in advance of the item being taken up in the House. At the request of leaders of opposition groups it has also been arranged that Members in whose name the item appears in the list of Business are supplied with a copy each of the statement if necessary in the House, before the item is taken up.

When admitting a Calling Attention, an enquiry may be made from the Minister regarding his convenience to make the statement but this is not obligatory on the Speaker. A Minister cannot refuse to make the statement when his attention is called but in case he does not have the requisite information, he can ask for time to make the statement. Accordingly, on the day to which the item has been postponed, the Minister makes the statement straight away without his attention being called again and thereafter members in whose names the item had been put down ask clarificatory questions.

After Minister makes statement in response to Calling Attention, members whose names appear in the list of Business are allowed to ask a clarificatory question each and the Minister replies thereto.

The statements made in response to Calling Attention have a wide scope. Such statements apart from giving factual information, often include opinions, conclusions, and decisions of the Government over which there need not be complete agreement on all sides of the House. At times the Minister's statement also does not contain the full information. As a consequence to that, questions by members contain prefaces, criticism for not giving full information, arguments in support of or against opinions, conclusions and decisions of Government mentioned in Minister's statement and at the end a few specific questions which are presented as parts (a), (b) etc. Several

Attempts have been made to prescribe time limit within which the item regarding Calling Attention should be disposed of. Now it is decided that the Member who calls attention, should not take more than ten minutes and the other four members not more than five minutes each. The Minister may reply at the end to all the questions asked by the members and the total time taken on a Calling Attention on a day should be restricted to half an hour to forty-five minutes. An announcement to this effect was made in the House on 18th November 1985. The revised procedure is working well.

A procedure sometimes adopted to save the time of the House is that where the statement by the Minister is lengthy, say exceeding three or four pages, instead of reading it to the House *in toto*, either the Minister lays it on the Table or give a brief summary thereof and lays the full text on the Table. As copies of the Statement are made available to members concerned in advance, members can ask clarificatory questions immediately thereafter.

Statement by Minister

Under rule 372 of the Rules of procedure and Conduct of Business in Lok Sabha, statement may be made by a Minister on a matter of public importance with the consent of the Speaker. Notice of Minister's intention to make a statement in the House has normally to be sent to Lok Sabha Secretariat at least two days in advance so that there is sufficient time for the Speaker to take a decision and to include that item in the list of Business. Where it becomes necessary for a Minister to make a statement in Lok Sabha at a short notice due to sudden accident or happening or where a statement to be made is of a secret nature and inclusion of the item in the list of Business will leak out the subject of the statement, the Minister concerned has to write to the Speaker and seek his permission to make the statement without entry in the list of Business.

Such statements are usually made after the Question Hour and laying of papers on the Table. Therefore, on the day on which a Minister has to make a statement in the House, he has to be present in the House a little before the termination of the Question Hour.

At times requests are received from certain Ministers for making statements at certain fixed hours. Such requests are usually not acceded to as it is not possible to interrupt the business before the House in between to allow the Minister to make the statement. Ministers are allowed to make statements after the Question Hour or at the end of the sitting of the day.

Whenever Minister has to make a statement, 150 copies of the statement in English and 100 copies of the statement in Hindi are required to be supplied by the Ministry to the Lok Sabha Secretariat at 10.00 A.M. on the day on which the statement is to be made. Where, however, the required number of the cyclostyled copies of the Statement are not available in advance, the Ministries are required to supply at least, six copies of the statement in addition to one copy for Interpreters Branch before the commencement of the sitting. In case the request for making the statement is sent at short notice two copies of the statement to be made by the Minister are required to be sent along with the communication seeking permission to make the statement. Thereafter, the requisite number of copies of the statement should be sent by at least half an hour before the statement is actually made. These copies are made available to members in advance through the Parliamentary Notice Office except when the statement is of a secret nature.

No questions are permitted to be asked at the time a statement is made in the House. If members want to raise a discussion on the statement, they have to give notice of a motion under Rule 184 or of short duration discussion under Rule 193.

Notice Regarding Inaccuracies in Information given by Ministers

A member may, under direction 115, with the prior permission of the Speaker, focus the attention of the House to any mistake or inaccuracy in a statement made by a Minister or any other member on the floor of the House, if the matter so challenged has an intimate relation to his own statement or arises out of a question asked by him. A member wishing to point out such a mistake or inaccuracy has to write to the speaker pointing out the particulars of the mistake or inaccuracy and seek his permission to raise the matter in the House. This procedure is applicable to information given in statements, information given during the debate as also information given in reply to answers to questions. The member may place before the speaker such evidence as he may have in support of his allegation. A copy of such a notice is usually sent to the Minister concerned for the purpose of ascertaining the factual position in regard to the allegation made. Comments of the Ministers on such notices are required to be sent as expeditiously as possible became in many cases members interrupt the businesses of the House to find out what has happened to their notices. Where a Minister finds that some time would be taken in ascertaining facts and furnishing the Minister's comments, an interim reply should immediately indicating sent, indicating the date by which the final reply would be sent. While sending the comments it should always be inicated whether there is any objection to a copy thereof being given to the member concerned. On receipt of Minister's comments, the matter is examined to find out whether there is any inaccuracy in the information given to the House or the matter needs clarification on the floor of the House. In either case the speaker permits the member to make a statement in the House and the member is asked to furnish text of the statement which he would make in the House. On receipt, the statement is examined and in case the Speaker finds that it contains any portions which are objectionable, unparliamentary or beyond scope of such statements, the member is asked to delete these portions. A copy of the statement as approved by the Speaker is forwarded to the Minister and he is required to make a statement in reply thereto and furnish a copy thereof in advance for Speaker's approval. The date for putting down the item is fixed in consultation with the member and the Minister, and entry made in the list of Business. After statements have been made by the Member and the Minister, no further debate is allowed and the matter is treated as closed. On the day on which the Minister is to make the statement in the House, 150 copies thereof in English and 100 copies in Hindi are required to be supplied to the Lok Sabha Secretariat by 10.00 a.m.

A Minister may make a statement *suo-moto* correcting the information given to the House but notice of Minister's intention should be sent before the member's notice is referred to the Minister. In case Minister gives notice after member's notice has been received by him. the Speaker usually directs the statement to be made in reply to member's statement.

Where notice of a member for pointing out inaccuracy in Minister's statement is disallowed on the basis of clarification given by the Minister in his note to the Speaker, the Speaker while disallowing the notice may direct that a copy of the Minister's note may be given to the member with Minister's consent or the facts furnished by the Minister conveyed to the Member.

Notice Under Rule 377

Matters, which are not points of order or which cannot be raised under the rules relating to Questions, Short Notice Questions, Calling Attention Motions etc. can be raised under Rule 377. This procedural device provides another opportunity to the members to make statements on matters of general public interests.

Notice for raising a matter under Rule 377 is to be given by a Member in writing addressed to the Secretary-General. Standard printed forms for giving notices are available in P.N.O.* The text of the statement proposed to be made should not ordinarily exceed 250 words. No matter can be raised unless the Speaker has given his consent thereto and only the approved text would go no record.

Notice for raising matters under Rule 377 can be tabled from the date specified in Bulletin Part-II circulated along with the summons for the session. Normally the notices are entertained three clear days before the commencement of the session. Notices should be given by 10.00 hrs. Notices received after 10.00 hrs. on a day are deemed to have been given for the next sitting of the House. It is, however, not necessary that notices given for a particular day will be allowed to be raised at a sitting. Notices received at the same point of time on a day are balloted to determine their *inter-se* priority.

All notices under Rule 377 are valid for the week in which these have been tabled. Notices received up to 10.00 hrs. on the last day of the week on which the House sits and not selected automatically lapse. However, such notices can be revived for the following week.

The notices for the following week can be given only after 10.00 hrs. on the last day of the week on which the House sits and are valid for the entire following week. In order to obviate inconvenience to Members, all notices given after 10.00 hrs. and upto 10.30 hrs. on the last day of the week on which the House sits, are deemed to have been received at the same point of time and these are balloted together to determine the *inter-se* priority of Members. Notices received subsequently are arranged in accordance with the date and time of their receipt.

If a notice is to be admissible, it must satisfy *inter alia* the following main conditions—

(1) It should raise substantially one definite issue;

(2) It should not raise an issue which does not fall within the Union Government's Jurisdiction that is to say, Union Government's responsibility should be clearly attracted;

(3) It should not contain allegations of a defamatory or incriminatory nature;

(4) It should not be on a subject on which a Question/Calling Attention Motion etc. has been discussed or admitted;

(5) It should not raise purely local issue or be of concern to some individual(s); and

* Parliament Notice Office.

(6) It should not relate to a matter which is sub-judice.

A copy of the text as approved by the Speaker is provided to the Member on the day on which he is allowed to raise the Matter. The item is not included in the list of Business. However, it is generally taken up after Calling Attention. On days when there is no Calling Attention on the agenda, the item is taken up immediately after papers have been laid and Bills, if any, introduced. A member can raise only one matter during a week under Rule 377.

On the day (usually Friday) when the Minister of Parliamentary Affairs makes a statement regarding Government Business, matters under Rule 377 are not raised.

Normally, Ministers do not make statements in response to matters raised under Rule 377. However, if a Minister so desires he may make a statement on the subject with the permission of the Speaker. The Ministers write to the Members with regard to matters raised by them under Rule 377, informing them of Government's view and/or action taken in the matter. Further clarification, if any, may be obtained by members directly from the Minister/Ministry concerned.

Requests from Members

On the last sitting of the week (usually Friday) when the Minister of Parliamentary Affairs makes a statement regarding Government Business for the following week, members (not more than 10, other than those who are Members of the Business Advisory Committee), are permitted to make submission for inclusion of their items in the next week's agenda. Members are required to give notice in writing before 10.00 a.m. on the day on which the statement is to be made indicating not more than two points which they wish to make. As only ten members are permitted to make submissions, all valid notices are balloted to select the names of ten members to determine their *inter-se* priority.

Text of submissions proposed to be made, should be brief, not exceeding 250 words, precise and pertain to matters coming within the purview of Central Government and should be forwarded along with the written communication to the Secretary-General. These should not be allegatory in nature.

This provides the members an opportunity to focus the attention of the House on matters of public interest which are agitating their minds and which they want to be discussed in the House.

The Question-Hour

Asking of questions is considered a Parliamentary right of all the members irrespective of their party affiliations. Hence, every member, whether, belonging to the ruling party or in the opposition is entitled to ask questions. Members can ask questions on different aspects of administration and governmental activity. Questions are to be addressed to a Minister for the purpose of eliciting information on a matter of public importance within the special cognizance of that Minister.

Although the apparent purpose of asking a question is to elicit information, the real object of the member is to point out the shortcomings of administration, to ascertain the thinking of the Government on a particular matter or even to give information to help the Government in formulating their policy and where the policy already exists, in making suitable modifications in that policy.

During the hour usually twenty questions are slated for oral answer. In case there are many questions, a ballot is taken by means of a randum sample. A Member who asks question can ask two supplementaries and others only two more from both sides of the House.

Thus, answers to questions achieve twin objective—one, the public at large come to know of the policies of the Government; two information about public reaction and public opinion about a Government policy and its implementation including its shortcomings is fed back to the Government to enable them to make necessary modifications, if so required in the public interest. There have been a number of instances in the past when persistent questioning on a particular matter revealed the misuse of public funds and abuse of authority.

Sometimes repartees full of wit and humour abound in the Question Hour. Ministers doing their home work are better equipped to face the questions as well as the volley of supplementaries which throw a searchlight on the working of administration.

The Question Hour enjoys a special place in the parliamentary proceedings. Perhaps this is the only parliamentary device which is made use of by most of the members of the House and so often. Because of the large attendance of the members as well as Ministers during the Question Hour, the prominent importance of this device, among other parliamentary devices, is the sure and effective method of obtaining information on a variety of matters concerning administration. The sharp, witty and humorous exchanges during the Question Hour provide a wide attraction to the Press as well as public in the galleries of the Hour and outside. Of late, live telecast of Question Hour has also been started.

Grouping of Ministries and Types of Questions

For the purpose of answering questions in Lok-Sabha, the Ministries and Departments of the Government of India are divided into five group—A, B, C, D and E and these groups of Ministries have been allotted Mondays, Tuesdays, Wednesdays, Thursdays, and Fridays respectively. The grouping is done in such a way that each Minister has one fixed day in a week for answering questions in Lok Sabha and another fixed day in the week for answering questions in Rajya Sabha. If, however, there is no sitting of the House on any of the above five days on account of a holiday, the questions pertaining to the Group of Ministries fixed for that day are not put down for answer in that week.

The grouping of the Ministries/Departments of the Government of India for answering questions for a particular session may be along the pattern hypothesised below.

Group A (Monday)	:	Agriculture; Information and Broadcasting, Labour, Steel & Mines; Urban Development.
Group B (Tuesday)	:	Communications; Energy; Industry; Law and Justice; Petroleum and Natural Gas; Food and Civil Supplies; Parliamentary Affairs.
Group C (Wednesday)	:	Prime Minister; Atomic Energy; Defence; Electronics; Environment and Forests; Ocean Development; Personnel, Public Grievances and Pensions Planning; Science and Technology; Space; Home Affairs; Programme Implementation; Welfare.
Group D (Thursday)	:	Health and Family Welfare, Human Resource Development; Transport; Water Resources.
Group E (Friday)	:	Commerce; External Affairs; Finance; Tourism; Textiles.

Grouping is changed according to the changes in the re-structuring of Ministries or re-shuffle in portfolios or some other valid reasons. In each group of Ministries, there are some important Ministries about which more questions are tabled. Grouping is done in such a way that as far as practicable, each group has approximately the same number of questions. The Ministries which attract large number of questions are not usually bunched together; one or two such Ministries are normally put along with other Ministries which attract lesser number of questions.

Requests are sometimes received from a Minister of Parliamentary Affairs. There are examined and, with the approval of the Speaker, the Ministry is taken out from one particular Group to another and as a result thereof the Ministry in the latter Group which attracts nearabout the same number of Questions is taken out from that Group and placed in the Group where the vacancy occurred. Otherwise, some other inter changes are made to keep a balance. This of course is done whenever possible in consultation with the Ministers involved.

In the Rajya Sabha also a similar method in followed. Whenever a change is made in the grouping of Ministries in Lok Sabha a similar regrouping is done in Rajya Sabha also.

The Rules of procedudre and conduct of Business in Lok Sabha provide that unless the Speaker otherwise directs, the first hour of every sitting shall be available for the asking and answering of questions. Similar provision is contained in Rule 38 of the Rules of Procedure and Conduct of Business in Rajya Sabha. This first hour is known as the Question Hour.

The Question Hour starts at 11.00 a.m. in the morning and concludes at 12.00 Noon on five days in a week when the House sits i.e. Monday, Tuesday, Wednesday, Thursday and Friday. In case any business like oaths by members or obituary references etc. are taken up at 11.00 a.m. the time taken thereon is not made good by extending the Question Hour beyond 12.00 Noon. Normally on Saturdays there is no suiting of the Lok Sabha (or Rajya Sabha). However, if a sitting on a Saturday is fixed it is without Question Hour. Normally, Question Hour is not similarly, fixed during the extending period of a Session

Lok Sabha Questions with which Ministries are concerned are of four types:

(1) *Starred Questions*

These are Questions, answers to which are desired orally on the floor of the House during Question Hour. These are distinguished by an asterisk.

(2) *Unstarred Questions*

These are Questions to which written answers are given by Ministries which are deemed to have been laid on the Table of the House at the end of the Question Hour and printed in the day's proceedings (Debates) of the House.

(3) *Short Notice Questions*

Questions which can be asked orally in the House after Question Hour at a notice shorter than prescribed for starred and Unstarred Questions. These must relate to a subject matter considered by the Speaker to be of urgent public importance. Short Notice Questions can be taken up even on the days when there is no Question Hour.

(4) *Supplementary Questions*

Which arise out of a starred or short notice question and the Minister's answer thereto can be asked with the Chair's permission immediately after the Minister has answered the main question, for the purpose of further elucidating any matter of fact.

In Lok Sabha, the list of starred Questions is printed on green paper, the list of Unstarred Questions on white paper, and the list of short Notice Questions on pink paper.

In Rajya Sabha the list of Starred Questions is printed on pink paper, the list of Unstarred Questions on yellow paper and the list of short Notice Questions on white paper.

Notices of Questions

A member has to give minimum 10 clear days' notice of a Question. The maximum period of notice prescribed in the Rules is 21 clear days but members can give notices of questions from the day following the day on which summons are issued. In order to determine the *inter se* priority of questions, all notices of Starred and Unstarred Questions received up to 10.00 a.m. on the 21st day before the date of answering the questions are deemed to have been received at 10.00 a.m. on the 21st day and balloted separately. Separate ballots are held of notices of Starred and unstarred Questions for each sitting. Thereafter these are diarised and separate serial numbers are alloted to Starred and Unstarred Questions on the basis of the position secured by members giving notices in the ballot and the order of preference given by them. All notices received after the ballot are diarised serially according to the time of their receipt in the Secretariat.

A member can give as many notices of questions as he likes for a particular day but the total number of questions that can be put down in his name in the list of Questions, both Starred and Unstarred together for a day cannot exceed five. The total number of Questions in the Starred list for a day is normally 20 and not more than one question of a member can be included therein. This may, however, be exceeded by the number of transferred or postponed questions added to the list.

In order to enable the members to address their questions to the correct Ministers, a booklet "Government of India—Demarcation of Responsibilities—Subjects for which different Ministries and Departments of Government of India are responsible" is brought out by the Lok Sabha Secretariat at the begining of each Lok Sabha and as and when it becomes necessary owing to substantial changes in the allocation of business to Ministries. This booklet is based on the information furnished by the Cabinet Secretariat. Corrections and changes in this booklet are printed as addendum to the publication and circulated to members.

Admissibility of Questions

The admissibility of questions in Lok Sabha is governed by Rules 32 to 54 of the Rules of Procedure and Conduct of Business in Lok Sabha. The admissibility of Questions in Rajya Sabha is governed by Rules 38 to 50 of the Rules of Procedure and Conduct of Business in Rajya Sabha.

Notices of questions are also given by member in pursuance of assurances given in reply to questions answered earlier in Lok Sabha. In such cases it is first ascertained whether statement in fulfilment of the assurance has already been laid on Table. In case the statement has been laid, the question is disallowed and attention of member is invited to the statement. When, however, no such statement has been laid on the Table and a period of more than three months from the date of giving the assurance has elapsed, the question is admitted as the Committee on Government Assurances have laid down a period of three months for the implementation of assurances.

With regard to questions based on newspaper reports, as far as possible, names of the papers are not allowed even though mentioned by the member in the notice. However, in order to enable Ministries to prepare the answer, in the provisionally admitted copy to the questions, the name and date of newspaper may remain. Ministries collect advance copies of provisionally admitted questions from the Distribution Branch of the Lok Sabha/Rajya Sabha Secretariat.

From time to time the Lok Sabha Secretariat receives intimation that particular Ministers are going to make statements on the floor of the Lok Sabha in regard to certain matters such as floods, natural calamities or some incidents that have taken place. Notices of Questions relating to such subjects are kept pending and after the statement is made, the questions are examined to see if they are covered; otherwise they are admitted.

Questions on Statutory Corporations

The admissibility of questions relating to Statutory Corporations and limited companies in which Government have financial or controlling interest is usually considered according to established practices and precedents. Where the subject matter relates to a matter of policy or an act of ommission or the question raises, a matter of public interest, the question is admitted. A question which relates to day-to-day administration or tends to throw work on the Corporation not commensurate with the results to be achieved, is normally disallowed.

Sometimes questions are asked seeking information on matters relating to States. When the States are under President's Rules, all questions pertaining to matters falling within the sphere of that State are admitted. In other cases, questions simply requiring information without touching the policy or the administration of a state are usually admitted, but questions seeking information on matters wholly within the State autonomy, in respect of which the State Governments have no concern with Union Government and are not responsible to it in law or fact, are not admitted. However, questions touching the policies of the State Administration which relate to the following are admitted:

— Action taken on all-India basis;
— Matter of all-India importance, *e.g.* Boundary-disputes, Border incidents;
— Where Government of India give advice, *e.g.*—Rail-road coordination, research institutes, etc.
— Where State Governments are agents of the Central Government; *e.g.* Implementation of Grow More Food Campaign Scheme; and
— Matters relating to Scheduled Castes, Scheduled Tribes about which the Central Government have a special responsibility.

Usually the following types of questions are admitted for written answer, that is, as Unstarred Questions.

(1) Questions seeking information of statistical nature;

(2) Question seeking information in great detail;
(3) Question raising matters of local interest;
(4) Question relating to strength of staff in Govt. offices or Departments and representation in the service of communities protected under the constitution.
(5) Question on which *prima facie* there could be no scope of supplementaries;
(6) Question asking for statement to be laid on the table; and
(7) Question of interest only to a limited section of the people.

These, however, are only illustrative of the types of questions which may be admitted as unstarred, each question is considered on its individual merits.

In certain cases it becomes necessary to refer a question to the Ministry concerned to ascertain facts in the First instance. This is ordinarily done in the following circumstances :

(i) Where the responsibility of the Central Government is not clear;
(ii) Where the question *prima-facie* relates to a matter affecting security of the country;
(iii) Where the question is allegatory in nature;
(iv) Where the question is obscure or is of a technical nature; and
(v) Where relations with foreign countries are involved.

Ministers are requested to furnish this as well as other factual information to Lok Sabha Secretariat as early as possible but not later than two days after receipt of such references. Priority question (*i.e.* question tabled by members who have secured priority upto thirty in ballot and which are likely to be included in List of Question for oral answer) are typed on Special forms which indicate "Priority in Ballot" secured by the member tabling the notice and "Number of Notices" tabled by him. The order of preference, if any, given by the member to the question is typed on the form as OP-I, OP-II, etc. Inclusion of a question in the list of questions for oral answer depends upon the priority secured in the ballot, the order of preference indicated by him and the orders passed by the competent authority.

On receipt of a note from the Ministry, in response to reference made by the Lok Sabha Secretariat, the question is examined and thereafter admitted or disallowed. The discretion in admitting or disallowing questions is solely vested in the Speaker and he cannot share his responsibility in this matter with any other authority. Speaker also need not give reasons for disallowance of a question and his decision is final. Normally, when the Ministry takes the plea of public interest in refusing to disclose the information, the questions are generally admitted as the Minister has to take such plea on the floor of the House. The Rules as they stand do not permit disallowance of such question. If, however, on the grounds of larger national interest (prejudicial, to the safety of the State) a request is made to the Speaker with the approval of the Minister concerned well in time, the Speaker may consider disallowance of such a questions.

The rules relating to the admissibility of questions both in Lok Sabha and in Rajya Sabha are almost the same. However, there is one which lays down that a question shall not seek information about matters which are in their nature secret. Similar provision in the Lok Sabha does not exist. Such question in Lok Sabha are decided on merits as per practice.

According to Rajya Sabha rules, questions must be clearly and precisely expressed. Lok Sabha Rules do not have a similar provision, but questions which are vague in nature and are not clearly and precisely expressed for specific answer, are not admitted in Lok Sabha also.

Non-Admissible Questions

Questions containing arguments, inferences or defamatory statements or otherwise refer to the conduct or character of any person except in his official or public capacity are not admitted. Questions which are in substance repetitions of those that have been answered previously or in regard to which information is available in accessible documents or in ordinary works of references are not admitted. Besides, if the subject matter of a question is pending for judgement before any Court of law or any other tribunal or, body set up under the law is under consideration before a Parliamentary Committee, the same is not permitted to be asked. Questions making discourteous references to foreign countries with whom India has friendly relations are disallowed. Similarly, questions raising too large of issue of policy are not allowed for it is not possible to enunciate policies within the compass of an answer to a question.

Question Lists

After the last date of receipt of questions is over, the admitted questions are arranged in order of priority obtained by the members in ballot and the order of preference indicated on the notice. In putting down the questions in the list, OP-I questions of the members are included unless they have been admitted as Unstarred or disallowed or transferred. Where there is no question admitted as Starred from any of the Member securing position within 20, a question from the Member securing 21st position is put down in the list and so on.

All admitted questions which do not find a place in the Starred List of Questions are included in the Unstarred List of Question, subject to the condition that each Member has at least one question in his name and no member has more than five questions (both Starred and Unstarred together) on any one day and the total number of questions in the Unstarred list does not exceed 230. This number may be exceeded by 25 at the most if there are questions pertaining to states under President's Rule.

The Lists of Questions are printed both in English and Hindi. Translation of Questions included in the final Members lists are made from English to Hindi by Translation Branch in Lok Sabha Secretariat. The printed lists are circulated to Ministries, members and others, five clear days in advance of the date of answer.

Transfer/Postponement of Questions

Transfer of questions from one date to another is carried out through corrigenda on receipt of written acceptance from the Ministry concerned where the lists of questions have already been printed. Otherwise, they are transferred on orders passed on the file. Where the transfer is within the same group of Ministries, the date remains unchanged; only the name of the Ministry is changed. Otherwise, the question is included in the list of questions of the next date alloted for the Ministry accepting the transfer. Member/Ministries are always informed in writing about transfer of their questions in advance.

For postponement of a Starred Question printed in the list of Starred Questions on the ground that the Ministry has not been able to collect information or will not be able to collect information by the due date, the Minister concerned has to write to the Speaker in advance so that after Speaker agrees to it, the postponement can be given effect to through corrigenda. However, the postponed date has to be within the same session in which the Question was admitted. The convenience of member concerned to the date of postponement is also ascertained. Such requests have to be made at the earliest convenience of the Minister concerned. A copy of the letter from the Minister to the Speaker may be endorsed to the Chief Examiner of Questions and delivered by hand to facilitate the action by the Lok Sabha Secretariat.

Disallowed Questions

Question Branch issues a disallowance letter to the member concerned. In some cases, on reconsideration, disallowed question are admitted on representation from the member either in the same form or in an amended form. Ministries are not informed about disallowance in writing.

As per practice, the Parliament Assistants of Ministries keep a close liasion with the Question Branch of Lok Sabha/Rajya Sabha Secretariat about the position of admitted/disallowed questions. The printed list of Questions, circulated to Ministries is the final list on the basis of which Ministries answer the questions in the House.

Answer to Questions

While preparing answers to questions, Ministries are expected to keep in view these points.

Answers to questions given in the House shall be complete and, as far as possible each of its part shall be answered separately.

If the Speaker is satisfied that it does not fulfil the condition, he may direct the Minister to give a complete answer.

Sets of Answers

Five sets of answers are sent to the Press Gallary of Lok Sabha for use by selected Press Correspondents in the gallary and two sets for use by the Press and Public Relations Branch of the Secretariat. These answers are, however, not shown to the Press Correspondents until the Question Hour is over and these have been answered in the House or laid on the Table of the House.

Ten complete sets of English and Five sets of Hindi version of answers to Starred and Short Notice Questions included in a day's list are placed in the Parliamentary Notice Office an hour before the commencement of the Question Hour for reference by members in order to enable them to ask relevant supplementaries on the basis of replies to be given to these questions on the floor of the House. In addition, eight sets of answers to Starred Questions in English and four sets of answers in Hindi are placed in the outer lobby of the House for reference by members.

If the answer to a question is amended or revised by the Minister on the floor of the House, the earlier answer is substituted by the revised answer furnished by the Ministry in the sets and in the Debates.

Therefore, unless corrections or modifications made in the answers on the day on which the answer is to be given, are communicated by the Ministry concerned to the Lok Sabha Secretariat well in time, it is not possible to supply amended answer to the press in the Press Gallery of the Lok Sabha. This may result in complication.

When Question Hour is dispensed with owing to the cancellation of the sitting of the House or its adjournment without transacting any business, the questions entered in the List of Questions (both Starred and Unstarred) for that day are treated as Unstarred Questions for the next sitting and printed with their answers as such in the official report of that day. Therefore, even in such a situation the Ministries concerned have to send, as usual, the replies to the questions listed in advance of the day when the questions are due for answers.

When the Question Hour is dispensed with, but the sitting is not cancelled on that day, all questions listed for that day are treated as Unstarred and printed with their answers in the official report of that day.

Corrections

When a Minister wishes to correct any inaccuracy in the information which he has given in answer to a Starred/Unstarred/Short Notice Question or a Supplementary Question, the Minister has to follow the procedure laid down for the purpose.

Short Notice Questions

On receipt of a Short Notice Question it is examined to see if it relates to a recent matter of public importance which requires urgent attention. In order to decide whether the matter is urgent, a Short Notice Question may be referred to the Minister concerned for facts with covering note addressed to the Private Secretary to the Minister concerned, and copy thereof endorsed to the Ministry. Replies by Minister are to be sent at the earliest but not later than two days from the date of reference. If no reply is received, the question is submitted for disposal on merits of the notice. Where matter raised in the short Notice Question is, considered to be *prima facie* urgent, an enquiry is made from the Minister as to whether he is prepared to answer the question at Short notice. If the Minister regrets his inability to accept the short Notice Question, the question is either disallowed and

Member informed accordingly or it may be admitted as an ordinary question for answer with minimum ten clear days' notice. There is, however, provision in the Rules that if the Speaker is of opinion that a Short Notice Question which a Minister is unable to answer at short notice is of sufficient public importance to be orally answered in the House, he may direct that the question be placed as the first question on the List of Questions for the day on which it would be due for answer under the Rules. Ordinarily, not more than one such question on a day is given such priority.

Normally, only one Short Notice Question is put down for answer on one day where the Minister has agreed to accept a Short Notice Question and where the Speaker admits such a Question. A Short Notice Question may be answered even on a day at a sitting of the Houses having no question hour.

'Half - An - Hour' Discussion

Members can give notice under Rule 55(2) of the Rules of Procedure and Conduct of Business in Lok Sabha for raising discussion on a matter of sufficient public importance which has been the subject of a recent question, oral or written and the answer to which needs elucidation on a matter of fact.

The discussions, if admitted are limited to half-an-hour and are held in the last half-an-hour of a sitting. Such discussions are held only on three sittings in a week, that is, on Mondays, Wednesdays and Fridays.

A Member wishing to raise half-an-hour discussion has to give notice in writing at least three days in advance of the day on which the discussion is desired to be raised. He has to specify in the notice the date on which he desires to raise the Discussions, the points on which elucidation is required, the question number and date whose reply needs further elucidation. The notice should also be accompanied by an explanatory note stating the reasons for raising discussion and should be signed.

The notices are carefully scrutinised and the following points are examined with reference to the original reply given to the questions and supplementaries thereon:

(a) whether the points intended to be raised by the member arise out of the answer to the relevant question;
(b) whether the period of notice satisfies the requirements of Rule 55;

(c) whether the points desired to be raised have been specified and relate to a matter of fact; and

(d) whether the reasons stated justify a discussion being raised.

All notices admitted for a particular date are balloted and the notice of the member who secures the first priority in the ballot is put down for discussion on the relevant date after admission. When a notice is to be put down for discussion the Ministry concerned is informed and copies of the notice, explanatory note and points proposed to be raised by the member are sent to the Ministry. The private Secretary to the Minister concerned and the Ministry of Parliamentary Affairs are also informed. Necessary entry is made in the List of Business.

On the date when the discussion is to take place, the members given notice of their intention for asking clarificatory questions during the discussion for elucidation. Such notices are received upto 11.00 a.m. on that day. Only four members can ask one clarificatory question each apart from the member in whose name the notice stands. If requests are received from more than four members, a ballot is held to determine the names of the first four members.

Where half-an-hour Discussion is interrupted for want of quorum before the Minister could give a reply to the debate, an enquiry is made from the Minister concerned under directions of the Speaker with a view to ascertain whether he would like to lay a statement on the Table of the House in reply to the said discussion. Where a Minister proposes to lay a statement under Direction 19, further steps in the matter are taken for making entry in the List of Business and obtaining authenticated copies of the proposed statement.

Government Assurances Committee

Ministers always give assurances while replying to questions in the House or during discussions on Bills, Resolutions and Motions. The required information is at times to be supplied to the House later. In order to watch the implementation of such assurances on behalf of the House, the Lok Sabha constitutes a Committee on Government Assurances.

The functions of the Committee on Government assurances are, to scrutinise the assurances, promises, undertakings etc. given by Ministers from time to time on the floor of the House and to report on—

(a) whether such assurances, promises, undertakings etc. have been implemented; and if so to what extent;

(b) if implemented, whether such implementation has taken place with in the minimum time necessary for the purpose.

The strength of the Committee is fifteen and the term of office is one year—from first of June to 31st May in the following year. The members of the Committee are nominated by the Speaker. The Chairman is also appointed by the Speaker from amongst the members of the Committee.

The Lok Sabha Secretariat studies Lok Sabha Debates every day during the session and culls out therefrom the assurances, promises, etc. which have been given in reply to question or in the course of debates on Bills, resolutions etc. The Ministry of Parliamentary Affairs also does the same exercise independently and sends statements of assurances compiled by them to the Lok Sabha Secretariat. Both these are cross-checked with a view to ensuring that all assurances have been properly extracted and these assurances which have not been included by the Ministry of Parliamentary Affairs are referred to the Ministry for their comments and inclusion in the statement.

The Ministry of Parliamentary Affairs sends relevant statements to appropriate Ministries for implementation of the assurances.

Implementation of the assurances is to be carried out normally within a period of three months from the date of the assurances in pursuance of a decision of the Committee on Government Assurances contained in para 6 of their Seventh Report, Fourth Lok Sabha. The Ministries go on sending statements in implementation of the assurances to the Ministry of Parliamentary Affairs from time to time. That Ministry consolidates these statements are the Minister lays them on the Table of the House usually twice during each session of the Lok Sabha, once at the begining and once towards the end. There is, however, always a time lag between the information supplied by the Ministry concerned to Ministry of Parliamentary Affairs and its being laid on the Table.

A statement is laid on the table and till then assurance is not treated as implemented. This task has been assigned to the Ministry of Parliamentary Affairs after a decision taken in January 1950. Therefore, if any information, reference, statements, etc. relating to assurances is received from the Ministries in the Lok Sabha Secretariat, they are passed on or referred to the Ministry of Parliamentary Affairs for necessary action.

Minister of Parliamentary Affairs lays the details about action taken in the House these are examined by the Lok Sabha Secretariat to see whether these have been implemented fully or not and if implemented whether it has been implemented within the prescribed period of three months. All pending assurances or assurances which have not been fully implemented are reviewed by the committee, from time to time. Apart from these, requests are also received from time to time, from the Ministries concerned through the Ministry of Parliamentary Affairs for dropping of certain assurances or for extension of time etc. These matters are also considered by the committee and their observation as incorporated in the reports which includes the minutes also are presented to the House by the Chairman or in his absence by a member of the committee. A peculiarly of the committee is that even though with the dissolution of the Lok Sabha, the Parliamentary slate is wiped clean, assurances pending before the dissolution of the Lok Sabha do not lapes and remain pending. Such assurances are considered by the committee constituted during the next Lok Sabha.

Processing of the Questions

Changes in the subjects dealt with by a Ministry or Department of Government of India, whether during the session or otherwise, should be communicated by the Ministries concerned to the Lok Sabha Secretariat immediately so that the information is kept up-to-date for the guidance of Members and the Secretariat.

Advance copies of provisionally admitted questions are forwarded to the Ministries concerned so that they may have more time for the collection of material for the preparation of answers. The Ministries are expected to examine the questions and any information etc. That the Ministry concerned may like to submit for consideration of the Speaker including the fact that the question lacks a factual basis should be forwarded to the secretariat as early as possible and in any case not later than three days from the date of receipt of the advance copies of the questions. If no communication is received witnin this period and after question has been put down on the order paper it will not be possihle to reconsider the admissibility of the question.

In case of the Short Notice Questions referred to Ministries for facts and/or acceptance, the comments on the questions may be sent to the Lok Sabha Secretariat within two days of the receipt of reference by them and should be addressed either to officer concerned of Lok Sabha Secretariat or by name or to the Question Branch.

The Ministries should move the appropriate Ministries for transfer of questions as soon as they receive advance copies of admitted questions and intimation regarding the acceptance of such transfers in writing by the accepting Ministries should be sent to the Lok Sabha Secretariat at the earliest. Where intimation regarding acceptance or transfer of a question is not received before the List of Starred Questions are sent to the printers, it is not possible to effect the transfer of questions from one Ministry to another from the printed list, particularly in the last week of the session. In such cases the Minister in whose name the question appears in the printed list of Starred Questions, has to answer the question.

The Question are addressed to the Ministers concerned who is supposed to answer them. But in some cases the Minister of State or Deputy Minister is to answer the question orally on the order paper. In such cases information regarding the person who will be answering questions on the order paper must be furnished to the Lok Sabha Secretariat by 3.00 p.m. on the working day preceding the date of answer of the relevant question.

When a Minister wishes to correct any inaccuracy in the information which he has furnished in reply to a Starred or Short Notice Question he should, ordinarily within one week, give to the Secretary-General, Lok Sabha notice of his intention to make a statement enclosing therewith a copy each of the statement in English and Hindi versions. One hundred and fifty copies of the statement along with two copies each of the statement in English and Hindi versions duly authenticated by the Minister should be sent to the Lok Sabha Secretariat by 5.00 p.m. atleast a day in advance.

As per convention, lengthy answers to Starred Questions are not to be read, but should be laid on the Table of the House.

Language

When Questions, the original notices of which are given in Hindi are received, the Hindi text of the questions should be considered as authentic and replies to such questions should be framed by Ministries on the basis of the Hindi text. In case of any doubt between the English translation and Hindi text of the questions, the Ministries should make a reference to the Lok Sabha Secretariat so that necessary clarification could be given if necessary after consulting the Members concerned.

The following papers should reach the Lok Sabha Secretariat by 15.00 hrs. at the latest on the working day preceding the date on which the questions are due for answer:

(1) *Type of Question*		Numbers of copies of answeres to be supplied by the Ministries.
Starred and Short Notice Questions		
(a) Original Notices in English	-	English 150 Hindi 50
(b) Original Notices in Hindi	-	English 150 Hindi 50
Unstarred Questions		
(c) Original Notices in English	-	English 150 Hindi 50
(d) Original Notices in Hindi	-	English 150 Hindi 50

(2) 50 extra copies of statement to be laid on the Table of the House for supply to members concerned through the Parliamentary Notice Office Under Direction 13(1) of the Direction by the Speaker.

(3) 50 extra copies of replies to previous Starred, Unstarred or Short Notice Question referred to in answers to questions for supply to Members concerned through the Parliamentary Notice Office, under the aforesaid Directions.

The Documents referred to in paras (2) and (3) above should be sent to Lok Sabha Secretariat in a separate cover marked "For Question Branch" with a forwarding note.

Copies of statement to be laid on the Table in reply to Starred Questions should be supplied both in English and Hindi.

Where the original notice of a question has been given by the Members of HIndi, the English version of the answer thereof should be cyclostyled on the backside of the same sheet as far as possible.

In the copies of the main answers to questions, the port-folios of the Ministers should be indicated in the following manner:

(i) The Minister of ______________ (Shri ______________)
(ii) The Minister of State in the Ministry of ____ (Shri _______)
(iii) The Deputy Minister in the Ministry of ____ (Shri _______)

Whenever in answer to a question a reference is made to a statement being laid on the Table, the fact should invariably be indicated thus ________ " ____________ statement is laid on the Table of the Lok Sabha".

All such statements should be provided with suitable and comprehensive subject headings.

The format of the replies should be uniform.

The format is as given below:

Lok-Sabha

Starred Question No. ______________

Unstarred Question No. ______________

To be answered on ______________ (Date)

(Subject of the Question)

Question No. ______________

(If Starred, an asterisk is given*) Name of the Member.

(Text of the Question)

Answer

Designation of the Minister (Name of the Minister)

English English

Hindi Hindi

(Text of the Answer)

3

PARLIAMENT'S CONTROL ON LAW-MAKING AND NATIONAL FINANCE

The Law Making Power

Parliament has wide legislative powers. The distribution of powers between the Union and the States is as per the provisions in the Seventh Schedule of the Constitution which contains three lists.

List-I enumerates the subjects on which Parliament alone can make laws. List-II enumerates the subjects on which the state legislatures alone can make laws. List-III is the concurrent list on which both the Parliament and the legislatures of States can make laws, but in the event of conflict between the two, the law made by the Parliament would prevail. The state legislatures have complete autonomy in matters under their jurisdiction; but the Residuary power i.e. any residual matter which does not clearly fall within any list or a new one, falls within the purview of Parliament. In spite of the wide range of subjects allotted to it in the Seventh Schedule of the Constitution, the Parliament can, under certain circumstances, assume legislative power over a subject falling within the sphere exclusively reserved for the states even in normal times. For example, Parliament may legislate on a matter included in the state list if Rajya Sabha declares , by a resolution supported by a two-thirds majority, that it is necessary or expedient in the national interest to do so. However, such a permission can be given only for one year at a time .

When a proclamation of emergency is made by the President, Parliament acquires the power to make laws with respect to any of the matters enumerated in the state list. Similarly, in the event of breakdown of the Constitutional machinery in a state, the powers of the legislature of that state may be exercised by or under the authority of Parliament under a Proclamation of Emergency by the President. The process of law-making is more or less the same in state legislatures as in Parliament, except in some cases, where a state proposes to enact a law it may under certain conditions specified in the Constitution he required to obtain the prior approval of the President for enacting such a law.

The Constituent Power

The power to amend the Constitution also rests with the Parliament except for some specific Articles, for amending which ratification by 50 per cent of the State legislatures is essential in addition to the special majority in both Houses of Parliament. If the amendment is passed in each House separately by the majority of the total Membership of the House and by the two-thirds majority of the present and voting Members it is considered as a special majority.

The Bills

A Bill is a blue print of the proposed enactment for the consideration, deliberation and assent of the House(s). Usually it originates from the Secretariat though the ideas and objectives may have come from the Ministry as a matter of policy. As such, drafting of a Bill is matter of skill and expertise which depends upon:

(a) knowledge of the subject-matter of the Bill,
(b) exact and precise understanding of the objects,
(c) mastery over language and power of expression, in accurate words and unambiguous phrase,
(d) knowledge of legal vocabulary—but which is understandable by men with ordinary intelligence.

The Bill should not have loopholes which may give rise to mischief.

The lay or immature politicians and the trained, seasoned civil servants jointly work upon the Bills to make them true to the spirit and objectives and foolproof.

The Bills are of various types. These are:

(a) Common or Ordinary Bills,
(b) Money Bills and Finance Bills, and
(c) Constitution Amendment Bills.

The Common or Ordinary Bills either seek to initiate new legislative proposals based on new policies, ideas, or to make new laws, amend or revise or even to repeal existing laws or to consolidate laws etc.

The Money-Bills and Finance-Bills form a different category of Bills as these can be introduced only with the prior consent of the President (naturally can be introduced only by a Minister), and they cannot originate in the Rajya Sabha.

The Bills containing matters specified in sub-clauses (a) to (g) of clause (1) of Article 110 of the Constitution are called Money Bills. In case a question arises whether a Bill is a Money Bill or not, the decision of the Speaker of Lok Sabha is final. A Money Bill contains the following matters :

(a) the imposition, abolition, remission, alteration or regulation of any tax;
(b) regulation of borrowings by the Government of India or any amendment pertaining to it;
(c) the custody or payments to or withdrawals from the Consolidated Fund of India or the Contingency Fund of India;
(d) the appropriation of moneys out of the Consolidated Fund of India;
(e) declaring of any expenditure to be expenditure charged on the Consolidated Fund of India increasing the amount of such expenditure. The expenditure charged on the Consolidated Fund of India includes items like, (a) the emoluments and allowances and other expenditure of the President; (b) the salaries and allowance of the Chairman and Dy. Chairman of Rajya Sabha and of Speaker and Dy. Speaker of the Lok Sabha; (c) Salaries and allowances of the judges of Supreme Court, High Courts, of the Comptroller & Auditor-General; and (d) expenditure on public debt, loans; sums to satisfy decrees, on awards of courts, or tribunals etc. (Expenditure charged on the Consolidated Fund of India is non-votable expenditure for the Parliament.)
(f) the receipt of moneys on account of the Consolidated Fund of India—the custody or issue of such money or the audit of the accounts of the Union or the States; and
(g) any matter incidental to any of the matters specified in sub-clauses (a) to (f) above.

An Appropriation Bill seeks to provide for the appropriation out of the Consolidated Fund of India of all moneys required to meet the grants made by the House of the People as well as the expenditure charged on the Consolidated Fund of India.

Constitution Amendment Bill

In India only the Union Parliament can initiate an amendment to the Constitution. The Bill may be introduced in either of the Houses but must be passed by a special majority in both Houses, separately. Joint meeting of the Houses cannot be called for this purpose. However, for amending some Articles, in addition to the special majority in the two Houses of Parliament, not-less-than-one-half of the state legislatures must ratify the amendments by making resolutions. These Articles pertain to the following:

(1) Election and the manner of election of the President (Arts. 54, 55) and the extent of the executive power of the Union and the States (Arts. 73 and 162).
(2) Art. 241, dealing with the High Courts in States or chapters dealing with Union Judiciary and High Courts in States.
(3) The Legislative relations between the Union and the States and any of the lists in Seventh Schedule.
(4) The representation of the States in Parliament.
(5) The provisions of Art. 368 dealing with the Amendment to the Constitution.

The Constitution makes a distinction between a Money Bill and a Finance Bill. A Finance Bill is a Bill making provision for any of the matters specified in sub-clauses (a) to (f) of clause (1) of Article 110 of the Constitution. It is presented along with the annual Budget. It relates to levying of new taxes or enhancing or reducing the existing taxes. These proposals become operative immediately after their presentation to Lok Sabha. Finance Bill ought to be passed or rejected before 1st of April i.e. begging of the new Financial Year.

Appropriation Bill and Finance Bill, both, are Money Bills.

The Law-Making Process

Preparation of a Bill

All legislative proposals must be brought in the form of Bills before the Parliament. It may be presented by a Government Member (i.e. a Minister) or a private Member of the House; and though it is passed by the Houses of Parliament it becomes law only after it receives the assent of the President. It is for this reason that some describe the President as the 'Third House'. Though the Bills come from the Government as well as the Private Members, the Government Bills which are important and more in number take the major portion of the Parliament's time.

A Bill originates as a legislative proposal and the Government Bills which are based on party policy or administrative requirements are initiated by a Ministry or the Minister. The Ministry concerned has to work out the political as well as administrative, financial, economic and social implications of the proposal. Opinion of the legal and constitutional experts is obtained through the Law Ministry or through Attorney-General. If necessary the concerned Ministries of the State Government are also consulted. After this scrutiny, a memorandum is submitted to the Cabinet for approval. The broad policy aspects are considered by the Cabinet and if found necessary it is referred to one of its Standing Committees. Later the Cabinet may approve the proposal.

The proposal is then converted into a Bill. This is a skilled job and is done by expert draftsmen. He must be given full information about the objects and purpose of the proposal, its exact connotation, and all relevant documents and information. He needs a good vocabulary of the technical terms, legal expressions and a command over language in general. Perfection in drafting the Bill depends upon his efforts. After the scrutiny of the Ministry or Cabinet it may have to be re-drafted.

A statement of objects and reasons is added at the beginning of the Bill which is the job of the concerned Ministry. It has to be in simple i.e. non-technical language which could be followed by a lay man. Certain other Notes, Memoranda etc. may also be appended to some Bills.

These may include the notes on clauses, financial memoranda, reasons explaining the reasons for making changes in the existing ordinance if any or in an Act; and the proposals to delegate the legislative powers through the Bill etc.

The Passage of a Bill

In India three readings of a Bill are considered essential. It is necessary that there is adequate scrutiny and discussion the Bill in every House. Out of the three readings the second reading is crucial while the first and the third do not offer much opportunity for a debate.

An ordinary Bill is introduced in either House of Parliament i.e.

in Lok Sabha or Rajya Sabha but a Money or Finance Bill can be introduced only in Lok Sabha.

The Minister who is to introduce a Bill has to give seven days notice in writing to the House about its introduction in the House. If the House grants permission it is introduced in the House which constitutes the First Reading of the Bill. If such an introduction is opposed (which is rare), the Speaker may ask the introducer as well as the Member who opposes to make statements.

Publication of the Bill in Gazette is done after its introduction in the House. However, with the permission of the Speaker it may be published before introduction in which case leave to introduce it need not be sought and it may be introduced straightway.

The most important stage is that of the Second reading. In its first stage the principle of the Bill and its provisions are discussed. The House may refer it to a Select Committee of the House or a Joint Select Committee of the Houses (in case of Money Bills) or it may be published for eliciting public opinion. If nothing is done, it is straight way taken for consideration.

The Select Committee Stage

This offers an opportunity for an objective and dispassionate consideration of the Bill *sans* party-limitation. Various interest groups or organisation who are likely to be affected are also consulted. Experts or experienced persons may also be called for evidence. Statistics may also be called for and studied. Clause-to-clause discussions are possible and some amendments can also be moved by Members of the Committee. Public opinion may be obtained through the State Governments also.

After the Select Committee stage, the second stage in the Second Reading is that of clause-by-clause discussion. The select Committee report/recommendations etc. are also taken up. Every clause, schedules etc. are discussed in detail in the House. Amendments are also moved at this stage: and if accepted by a majority of the present and voting Members, they are accepted. After the discussions are over if it is approved by the majority of members present and voting, it is accepted and Second Reading is over.

It is proposed by the Member who moved the Bill or the Member-in-charge that the Bill be passed (or with Amendments). At this stage there are no detailed discussions. Members may either speak in support of the Bill or oppose it. Only formal or verbal amendments or changes in a word or so are moved. If the Bill is passed by a simple molarity of the present and voting Members of the House it is deemed to be passed.

Only in case of the Constitution Amendment Bills special mojority i.e. a majority of the total Membership of the House and majority of not less than two thirds of the Members present and voting is required.

With the signature of the Secretary-General of the House it then goes to the other House.

The Bill then goes to the other House and it goes through the same stages and the three readings, except in case of the Money Bills.

The Money Bills, as already mentioned, can be introduced only in the Lok Sabha and after it is passed, it goes to the Rajya Sabha. Rajya Sabha may suggest amendments and return in within fourteen days from the date of its receipt. The Lok Sabha may accept or reject any or all the amendments/recommendations of the Rajya Sabha. Whether the Lok Sabha accepts or rejects the amendments or whether the Rajya Sabha passes the Bill or returns the Bill within the period of fourteen days or not, after the said period of fourteen days, it goes to the President for his consent as it is deemed to have been passed by both the Houses.

A joint meeting of both the Houses may be called by the President if an (ordinary) Bill is passed by either of the Houses and is pending consent in the other House and there is disagreement or dead lock between the Houses and six months have lapsed from the date of its receipt in the other House. The Speaker of Lok Sabha presides over such joint meeting. A decision is taken by majority vote.

Joint meeting cannot be called to consider the Constitution Amendment Bills.

After the Bill is passed by both the Houses of Parliament it is sent to the President for his assent. The Secretariat of the House which passed it last, obtains his assent, but in case it is passed at the Joint Sitting of the two Houses, the Lok Sabha Secretariat obtains it.

The President may grant his assent or return it with or without his recommendations for reconsideration. However, if the Houses pass the Bill with or without amendments and send it again for his assent, as per the provision in the Constitution, the President 'shall not withhold his assent', that means he has to give his assent. The same applies to a Constitutional amendment Bill.

It is only in case of a Money Bill that he cannot return it and has to give his assent after it is passed by the Houses. (As stated earlier, a Money Bill is introduced in Lok Sabha only after the prior assent of the President for its introduction.)

Previsions of Veto

From the above it is clear that the President can only delay his assent but cannot apply total veto. At the most it may be termed as a 'Suspensive Veto'. The ultimate power lies with the Parliament. Some writers on the Indian Constitution have referred to a 'Pocket-Veto' available to our President like that in the United States. This interpretation is based by them on the fact that the Indian Constitution does not prescribe any time-limit within which the President may either give his assent or return it with or without his recommendation. However, as per the informtion from the experts in Parliamentary practice in India and procedure from Parliament Secretariat, this does not affect the fate of the Bill. If the Bill is passed by both the Houses and is pending President's assent, it does not lapse even with the dissolution of the Lok Sabha. The time-limit for his assent is not prescribed, however once it is passed by the Houses and is pending with the President for his assent it never lapses irrespective of the time or dissolution of the House i.e. Lok Sabha. This shows that drawing an analogy with pocket-veto of the U.S. President is wrong.

During the Presidentship of Dr. Rajendra Prasad, the Hindu Code Bill was pending with the President as he had his own doubts on it. Later he gave his assent. During the Janata regime Shri N. Senjeva Reddy kept a Bill pending for a couple of days. The Postal Bill passed and sent during the Presidentship of Gyani Zail Singh (1987-88) was kept pending and after Shri R. Venkataraman became the President, he consulted legal experts and also sought opinion of the Attorney-General who expressed doubts about the constitutional validity of the law if passed. Later, during the tenure of the 9th Parliament the then government of Shri V.P. Singh took back the Bill.

The rules regarding lapsing of the Bill are stated below. If the Bill is passed by the Lok Sabha and is pending with the Rajya Sabha, if the Lok Sabha is dissolved, then the Bill lapses. The idea behind this rule is that the newly elected Lok Sabha should consider it afresh. On the contrary, if a Bill passed by Rajya Sabha is pending before the Lok Sabha and the Lok Sabha is dissolved the Bill does not lapse and the newly elected Lok Sabha can proceed with its consideration.

Private Members' Initiative in Legiaslation

Any Member who is not a Minister is a private Member. Though it is difficult, it is not impossible that Private Member's Bills are also enacted into Laws. After its introduction (approval of the Private Member's Bills Committee of the House) it is scrutinised by the concerned Ministry and Law Ministry and then it goes to the Parliamentary and legal Affairs Sub-Committee of the Cabinet. If not acceptable the reasons are explained before the House. However, many such Bills have become law or such Bills have prompted legal initiative on the part of Government. The examples of Bills which became law include:

— The Hindu Marriage (Amendment) Bills of 1956 and 1963.
— The Code of Criminal Procedure (Amendment) Bills of 1953 and 1957.
— The Muslim Wakfs Bill, 1952.
— The Marine Insurance Bill, 1963.
— The Ancient and Historical Monuments and Archaeological Sites and Remains (declaration of National importance) Bill, 1954.
— The Womens and Childrens Institutions (Licensing) Bill, 1954.
— The Indian Registration (Amendment) Bill, 1953.
— The Proceedings of Legislature (Protection of Publication) Bill, 1956.
— The Salaries and Allowances of Members of Parliament (Amendment) Bill, 1964.
— The Orphanages and other Charitable Homes (Supervision and Control) Bill, 1960.

Parliamentary Initative in Law-Making

Though the major portion of the legislative business come from the Executive, the Parliament does have its role and 'say' in legislation. It is not just a 'rubber stamp' or just a 'talking-shop'. After prolonged discussions it gives the final form and shape to the Bills introduced by the Executive. During the Committee stage, experts, organised interest groups etc. are also consulted. Public opinion is also consulted. Petitions from public on bills examined by Petitions Committee are also circulated to Members. During 1988, the Press Bill, purporting to curtail the freedom of the Press to publish charges of corrupt practices etc. was given up by the government due to heavy criticism from within and outside the House. Some legislative measures also originate from the Executive on the basis of Parliamentary opinion and suggestions.

Parliament's Control on National Finance

The Budget

Financial control of the Parliament is mainly through the Budget. Two budgets viz. the General Budget and Railway Budget, Demands for Grants and Excess Demands for Grants, Appropriation Bill and Finance Bill are the components of this control.

After the Budget is presented, Lok Sabha has opportunity for discussion on Financial proposals at several stages from the presentation of the Budget to the passing of Appropriation Bill and Finance Bill, as fallows:

(i) General discussion on the Budget,
(ii) Discussion and voting of Demands for Grants,
(iii) Consideration and passing of Appropriation Bill,
(iv) Cosideration and passing of Finance Bill.

In Rajya Sabha, financial proposals are discussed as under:

(i) General discussion on the Budget,
(ii) Consideration and passing of Appropriation Bill,
(iii) Consideration and passing of Finance Bill.

How is the Budget Presented ?

The Budget, which the Constitution terms as the annual Financial Statement containing the estimated receipts and expenditure of the Government of India in respect of a financial year, is laid before both the Houses of Parliament by the President, through Finance Minister.

The Budget is presented to Lok Sabha in two parts :

(i) Railway Budget pertaining to Railway finance; and
(ii) General Budget, which gives an over all picture of financial position of the Government of India excluding Railways.

It is since 1925 that the Railway Budget is being presented separately. The idea behind this separation was to secure stability for civil estimates by providing for an assured contribution from Railway revenues and also to introduce flexibility in the administration of the Railway finance. The Railway Convention Committee which is constituted from time to time recommends the rate of dividend payable by Railways to General Revenues. The recommendations of Railway Convention Committee in this regard are adopted through resolutions passed by Lok Sabha and Rajya Sabha.

The Railway Budget is presented in Lok Sabha by the Minister of Railways some time in the third week of February. The General Budget is presented to Lok Sabha by the Minister of Finance usually on the last working day of February at 5.00 p.m. However, in 1977, the General Budget for 1977-78 was presented at 12.55 hrs; as there were no new taxation proposals in the Budget. By the convention, on the day on which the General Budget is presented, Lok Sabha adjourns about an hour before presentation of the Budget and reassembles at 5.00 p.m.

In the year in which the general elections are held, the usual time schedule for presentation of Budget is not adhered to and necessary changes are made as regards the date of presentation of the Budget. In the years 1972 and 1976 also, which were not election years, this time schedule was not followed. In 1972, Railway Budget and General Budget were presented on 14th March 1972 and 16 March 1972, respectively. In 1976, Railway Budget and General Budget were presented on 10 March 1976 and 15 March 1976, respectively and the Railway Budget was presented on 16 June 1980. In 1991 the Railway Budget was presented on the 16th and General Budget on 24th July 1991 respectively. In 1997 the budget was presented in March 1997 but due to the no confidence motion passed against the Deve Gowda Ministry it could not be passed. Whether a special budget session should be held or not and whether a defeated Ministry's budget should be passed, became constitutional issues.

The Budget may be presented twice in an election year. In 1977, both the Railway and General Budgets were first presented on 28 March, 1977 and the General Budget on 17 June, 1977.

While presenting the Budget, the Minister concerned delivers his Budget Speech and lays on the Table the annual Financial Statement duly authenticated by him. There is no discussion on the Budget at that time. Simultaneously with the presentation of the Budget in Lok Sabha, a copy thereof is laid on the Table of Rajya Sabha.

The Railway Budget papers usually contain *inter alia* the following documents :

(a) Speech of Railway Minister introducing the Railway Budget,
(b) Budget of the Railway Revenue and Expenditure.
(c) Explanatory Memorandom on the Railway Budget.
(d) Demands for Grants.

(e) Works machinery and Rolling Stock Programmes.
(f) Indian Railways Report and Accounts, etc..

In the year 1982, for the first time the Railway Minister, following the pattern of the General Budget, delivered his speech, introducing the Railway Budget, in two Parts—Part-A and Part-B. Part-A contained the general survey of the Railway Finance and Part-B dealt with the Proposals for raising additional resources.

The Budget speech of the Finance Minister is in two Parts. Part-A of the Budget speech deals with the general economic survey and review of economic conditions in the year and the prospects in the following year. Part-B of the Budget speech contains budget proposals i.e. change in taxation and other sources of revenues for the coming financial year. Immediately after the presentation of the General Budget, the Finance Minister introduces in the Lok Sabha the Finance Bill to give effect to the proposals of the Government of India for the following financial year. The Bill contains proposals of the Govt. for levy of new taxes, modifications of the existing tax structure or continuance of the existing tax structure beyond the period approved by Parliament.

The General Budget papers usually contain *inter alia* the following documents:

(a) Speech of the Finance Minister—Part-A.
(b) Speech of the Finance Minister—Part-B
(c) Budget of the Central Government.
(d) Budget at a glance.
(e) Finance Bill.
(f) Memorandum explaining the provisions in the Finance Bill.
(g) Key to the Budget Documents.
(h) Explanatory Memorandum on the Budget.
(i) Summary of Demands for Grants.
(j) Demands for Grants in respect of various Ministries/Departments, etc.

Contents of the Budget

The Budget is presented to the House is such form as the Finance Minister may decide after considering the suggestions of the Estimates Committee.

The Estimates Committee of 1950-51 made certain suggestions, which were implemented by the Finance Minister in framing the

Budget. Again in 1972-73, the Estimates Committee made recommendations regarding revision of the form and contents of the demands for Grants.

The Budget contains three factors, namely—

(i) review of the Public Finance of the pervious year including the actual receipts and expenditure of that year;
(ii) estimate of the receipts and expenditure of the following year; and
(iii) proposals for meeting the requirements of the following year.

Accordingly, the Budget sets forth the receipts and the expenditure of the Government for three consecutive years. It gives—

(a) the actuals for the preceding year;
(b) the revised estimates for the current years; and
(c) the Budget estimates for the ensuing year.

Under the Constitution, Budget has to distinguish expenditure on revenue account from other expenditure. Government Budget, therefore, comprises of (i) Revenue Budget, and (ii) Capital Budget.

The Budget documents also exhibit broad break-up of expenditure plan and non-plan, sectorial allocation of plan outlays, and details of resources transferred by the Central Government to State and Union Territory Governments.

The General Budget is prepared by major Heads of Account prescribed in consultation with the comptroller and Auditor-General. The Budget statement shows the recipts and payments of the Government of India under the three parts in which Government Accounts are kept, namely—

(i) Consolidated Fund;
(ii) Contingency Fund; and
(iii) Public Account.

All revenues received by the Government of India, all loans raised by the Government, through issue of treasury bills, loans or ways and means advances and all moneys received by the Government in repayment of loans are credited to the Consolidated Fund of India. The Contingency Fund is an imprest placed at the disposal of President to meet urgent unforeseen expenditure pending authorisation by Parliament. Besides the normal receipts and expenditure of the

Governments which relate to the Consolidated Fund, certain other transactions enter Government account in respect of which Government acts more as a banker, for example, transactions relating to Provident Funds, Small Savings Collections, other deposits etc. The moneys thus received are kept in the Public Account and the connected disbursements are also made therefrom.

Under the Constitution, certain items of expenditure e.g. emoluments and allowances of the President, salaries and allowances of the Chairman and the Deputy Speaker of Lok Sabha, salaries, allowances and pensions of the judges of the Supreme Court and the Comptroller and Auditor-General of India, interest on the repayment of loans raised by Government and the Payment to satisfy decrees of Courts etc. are charged on the Consolidated Fund of India. The charged items are shown separately in the Annual Financial Statement.

Discussion on Budget

A day fixed by the Speaker, after the day of presentation of the budget, on which and for such time as the Speaker may allot, the House discusses the Budget as a whole or any question of principle involved therein, but no motion can be moved nor is the Budget submitted to the vote of the House at that stage. The Finance Minister has a general right to reply at the end of the discussion.

The scope of discussion at this stage is confined to general examination of Budget i.e. proper distribution of items of expenditure according to importance of a particular subject or service, policy of taxation as expressed in budget and speech of the Finance Minister and general scheme and/or deficit, revenue and expenditure accounts and the overall surplus or deficit. The method of estimation, whether revenue is overestimated or under-estimated, whether expenditure is pitched too high as also the division of taxation into direct and indirect taxation, can also be discussed but specific points or grievances can be dicussed when House takes up relevant Demands for Grants or the Finance Bill.

Vote on Account

Previously, after the presentation of the Budget and the introduction of the Finance Bill on the last day of February, both had to be passed before the financial year came to a close, that is the 31st March. This limited the time available to the House for a proper and satisfactory consideration of the Budget.

Since the whole process beginning with the presentation of the Budget and ending with discussion and voting on the Demands for Grants requires sufficiently long time, a provision has been made in the Constitution which empowers Lok Sabha to make any grant in advance in respect of the estimated expenditure for a part of any financial year pending the completion of the procedure for the voting of the demands for Grants and passing of the connected Appropriation Bill. This is known as 'Vote on Account'. The procedure regarding vote on Account was introduced for the fist time in Lok Sabha in the Budget session of 1951. The Chandra Shekhar Ministry sought a Vote on Account in February 1991 for 3 monthwise upto July 1991.

The purpose of a Vote on Account is to keep the Government functioning, pending the voting of final supply. It cannot be used normally as means of obtaining Parliamentary approval for 'new service' an assurance to the effect that provision obtained by Vote on Account will not be used for expenditure on 'new service' is, therefore, included by the Government in the introductory note to the Book of Demands relating to Vote on Account. Vote on Account states the total sum required, and the various amounts needed for each Ministry, Department or item of expenditure which compose that sum, are given in a schedule. The period covered by the Vote on Account is generally two months and the amount is approximately one-sixth of total Demands. In the election years, Vote on Account is taken for longer periods.

As the convention, Vote on Account is treated as a formal affair and passed by Lok Sabha without a discussion. It has been held that this convention is not in contravention of the provision of the Constitution. During the elections years, when Vote on Account is to be taken for a longer period, discussion has been allowed in the House.

Generally, Demands for Grants on Account are voted by Lok Sabha after general discussion on the Budget is over and before the detailed discussion on the Demands for Grants is entered upon. Ministry of Finance/Railways ensure that copies of the Books of Demands on account are supplied to the Lok Sabha Secretariat well in time for circulation to the Members.

Demands for Grants

The estimates of expenditure from the Consolidated Fund of India included in the Budget statement and required to be voted by Lok Sabha are submitted in the form of Demands for Grants. The Demands for Grants are not formally presented or laid on the Table of Lok Sabha. These form part of the Budget papers and are distributed to Members along with Budget documents. Each Demand first gives the total of 'voted' and 'charged' expenditure as also the 'revenue' and 'capital' expenditure included in the Demand separately and the grand total of the amount of expenditure for which Demand is presented. This is followed by the estimates of expenditure on each Programme/ organisation under 'plan' and 'non-plan' heads separately. The Demand for Grants incorporate Notes on Demands which give, in brief, the objectives of the Ministry/Department. Wherever possible, the targets and achievements in regard to major programmes are also given in these Notes. The Demands for Grants are followed by the detailed Demands for Grants which are laid on the Table of Lok Sabha some time after the presentation of the Budget, but before the discussion on Demands for Grants commences. The detailed Demands for Grants show further details of the provisions included in the Demands for Grants.

Separate Demands are ordinarily made in respect of the grants proposed for every Ministry. The Finance Minister may, include in one demand-grants proposed for two or more Ministries or Departments or make a Demand in respect of expenditure which cannot redially be classified under a particular Ministry. No Demand is made except on the recommendation of the President. The recommendation is communicated to the Secretary-General of Lok Sabha by the Minister concerned and is printed by the Ministry on the Books of Demands for Grants. Lok Sabha has power to assent, or to refuse to assent to any Demand or to assent, to any Demand subject to a reduction of the amount specified therein.

The estimates of expenditure charged on the Consolidated Fund of India are not submitted to the Vote of the House. The House has, however, every right to discuss the same. Members may also ask for any information relating to those items.

When the presentation of Budget is over, the Minister of Parliamentary Affairs holds a meeting of the leaders of Parties/Groups in Lok Sabha in regard to the selection and order of discussion of Demands for Grants of the Ministries which are to be discussed in the House and time to be allotted therefor. On the basis of the decisions arrived at this meeting Government forwards the proposals for the consideration of the Business Advisory Committee. The Business Advisory Committee after considering the proposals submitted by Government makes a report to the House. After adoption by the House of the report of the Committee, the allocation of time to various

Ministries whose Demands for Grants are to be discussed in the House, is published in the official Bulletin. The Minister of Parliamentary Affairs after consulting the programme and convenience of the Ministers concerned prepares a time-table showing the dates on which the Demands of the various Ministries would be taken up in the House and forwards the same to the Lok Sabha Secretariat. This is also published in Bulletin Part-II for the information of Members and Ministries. The Demands for Grants are not formally moved in the House by the Minister concerned. These are deemed to have been moved and are proposed from the Chair. The Minister may, if he so likes, initiate discussion on the Demands for Grants relating to his Ministry.

During discussion on Demands for Grants in respect of a Ministry, the debate is confined to a matter under the administrative control of that Ministry and to each head of the Demand as is put to the vote of the House. At the stage, it is open to Members to disapprove a policy pursued by a particular Ministry or to suggest measures of economy in the administration of the Ministry or to focus attention of the Ministry to specific local grievances.

Cut-Motions

The Demands for Grants are then discussed, motions can be moved for reducing the amount of any Demand for Grant. These motions are called Cut-Motion. A Cut-Motion is a device for initiating discussion on the Demands for Grants, so that the attention of the House is drawn to the matter specified in Cut-Motion. It is not necessary that discussion should start only on a Cut-Motion. The Cut-Motions are normally tabled by Members of the opposition. The members of the Ruling Party do not generally table such notices for it may amount to a vote of censure/against their own Government.

Cut-Motions may be of three types:

(i) Disapproval of Policy Cut,
(ii) Economy Cut, and
(iii) Token Cut.

---

* e.g. *Disapproval of Policy:*

That the Demand under the Head Ministry of External Affairs (Pages. . . .) be reduced by Rupee 1. — by Shri . . . . .

1. Failure to invoke total effective economic and political sanctions against Iraq as declared by the United Nations Assembly Resolution of February, 1991 calling the total isolation of Iraq.
2. Failure to order closure of Iraq's Consulate in Bombay despite U.N. General Assembly Resolution calling of total isolation of Iraq.

Disapproval of Policy Cut

The from of such a Cut-Motion representing disapproval of policy underlying the Demands is "that the amount of the Demand be reduced to Rupee 1".* The member giving notice of such a Cut-Motion indicates in precise terms the particulars of the policy which he proposes to discuss. The discussion is confined to the specific points mentioned in the notice and it is open to the Member to advocate an alternative policy.

Economy Cut

The format of such a Cut-Motion representing the economy that can be effected is, "that the amount of the demand be reduced by a specific amount."* The specified amount may be either a lump sum reduction in the Demand or omission or reduction of an item in the Demand. The Member giving notice indicates briefly and precisely the particular matter on which discussion is sought to be raised and his speech should be confined to the discussion as to haw economy can be affected.

Token Cut

The form of such a Cut-Motion seeking to ventilate a specific grievance which is within the sphere of responsibility of the Government of India, is "that the amount of the demand be reduced by Rs. 100." The discussion on such a motion is limited to a particular grievance specified in the motion.

Admissibility of Cut-Motions

A Cut-Motion in order to be admissible should satisfy the following conditions :

(a) It should relate to one demand only.
(b) It should be clearly expressed and should not contain arguments, inferences, ironical expressions, imputations and defamatory statements.

---

* e.g. *Economy*
That the Demand under the Head Indian Posts and Telegraphs Department (Page .....) be reduced by Rs. 19.000 . — by Shri .....

1. Location of the telephone exchange in a highly rented building at NGP.

(c) It should be confined to one specific matter which should be stated in precise terms.
(d) It should not reflect on the character or conduct of any person whose conduct can only be challenged on a substantive motion.
(e) It should not make suggestions for amendment.
(f) It should not refer to a matter which is not primarily the concern of the Govt. of India.
(g) It should not relate to a state subject or to matters which are not primarily the concern of the Govt. of India.
(h) It should not raise a question of privilege.
(i) It should not relate to expenditure 'charged' on the Consolidated Fund of India.
(j) It should not relate to a matter which is under adjudication by a court of law having jurisdiction in any part of India.
(k) It should not revive discussion on a matter which has been discussed in the same session and on which decision has been taken.
(l) It should not anticipate a matter which has been previously appointed for consideration in the same session.
(m) It should not ordinarily seek to raise a discussion on a matter pending before any statutory tribunal or statutory authority performing any judicial or quasi-judicial function or any commission or court of enquiry appointed to enquire into, or investigate any matter. However, the Speaker may in his discretion allow such matter being raised in the House as is concerned with the procedure or stage of enquiry, if the Speaker is satisfied it is not likely to prejudice the consideration of such matter by the statutory tribunal, statutory authority, commission or court of enquiry.
(n) It should not relate to a trifling matter.

The speaker decides whether a Cut-Motion is or is not admissible and may disallow any Cut-Motion when, in his opinion, it is an abuse of the right of moving Cut-Motion or is calculated to obstruct or prejudicially affect the procedure of the House , or is in contravention of the rules of Procedure of the House. It is a well established Parliamentary Convention that Cut-Motions seeking to discuss the action of the Chair or relating to Speaker's Department or matter under the control of Speaker are not allowed. Cut-Motion ventilating personal grievances and those casting aspersions on individual officials are not considered in order. Cut-Motions seeking to discuss the details of internal administration of an autonomous body are inadmissible.

There are some Cut-Motions making allegations against individuals but relating to a matter of public importance, which are allowed.

Cut-Motions relating to an alleged adverse impact of a certain action of the Government are admissible.

In one list, the Cut-Motions are grouped Demand-wise and under particular Demand, the disapproval of policy cuts come first, then the economy cuts, and thereafter the token cuts.

When the discussion on the Demands for Grants in respect of Particular Ministry commences, an announcement is made by the chair to the effect that Members who have tabled Cut-Motions in respect of the Demands of the Ministry may send slips to the Table indicating serial numbers of the Cut-Motions they would like to move and that those Cut-Motions would be treated as moved.

Ministries Reports

For the discussion on Demands for Grants of various Ministries/ Departments, copies of the Annual Reports of the working of the Ministries/Departments are supplied by Ministries/Departments concerned to the Lok Sabha Secretariat. Copies of the Annual Reports (both English and Hindi versions) are sent to the Lok Sabha Secretariat simultaneously by the Ministries concerned so as to reach not later than a week before the day the Demands for Grants of the concerned Ministry are taken up for discussion in Lok Sabha. On receipt of the Lok Sabha Secretariat, the copies of the Annual Reports are distributed to Members.

Performance Budgeting

With a view to make the Budget serve as a tool of management and also to enable better appreciation of the functioning of the various Ministries and Departments in Parliament and elsewhere, Performance Budgets are being presented by all the Ministries/Departments dealing in development activities with effect from the Budget Year 1975-76. The Performance Budget presents the Budget of the Ministries/ Departments or the origination, terms of functions, programmes and activities. The data included in the Performance Budget, besides explaining the scope and objectives of the programmes and schemes, give their estimated cost, and the purpose of the schemes, and the propose for which provisions are asked for in the revised estimates and budget estimates. Performance Budgets of the Ministries/ Departments also include performance-cum-programme statement relating to the various Public Sector Undertakings under the respective Ministries.

Copies of the Performance Budget of various Ministries/ Departments received from respective Ministry/Department are also circulated to Members.

Vote of the House

On the last day of the days allotted for discussion on the Demands for Grants at the time fixed in advance, the Speaker puts all the outstanding Demands for Grants to the vote of the House. This process is known as *Guillotine.* It is a device for bringing the debate on financial proposals to an end within a specified time. Consequently, several Demands have to be voted by the House without discussion. When the time for applying the Guillotine is reached, the Member or the Minister who is speaking in the House is asked by the Speaker to resume his seat. The Cut-Motions which have been moved are immediately put to vote and disposed of. Thereafter, the Demands for Grants which are under discussion are put to vote and disposed of. Ultimately all the outstanding Demands are guillotined.

Supplementary Grants

When the amount authorized to be spent for a particular service for the current financial year is found to be insufficient for the purposes of that year or when a need has arisen during the current financial year for supplementary or additional expenditure upon some 'new service' not contemplated in the Annual Financial Statement for that year, the President, through Minister, puts before both the Houses of Parliament another statement showing the estimated amount of that expenditure. The Demands for Supplementary Grants must be presented to, and passed by, the House before the end of the financial year.

Excess Demand

If money has been spent on any service during a financial year in excess of the amount granted for the service and for that year, the President causes to be presented to the House a Demand for such excess.

Demands for Excess Grants

Sometimes the amount granted for any service is found insufficient for the purpose during the financial year and the Government is compelled to spend the excess by withdrawal of money from the Contingency Fund of India in advance of sanction by Parliament. All cases involving such expenses are brought to the notice of Parliament by the Comptroller and Auditor-General through his report on the Apporpriation Accounts. The excesses are then examined by the Public Accounts Committee which makes recommendations regarding their regularisation in its report to the House. The Government thereafter presents to Lok Sabha the Demands for Excess Grants. The Demands for Excess Grants are presented to the House in the session in which the PAC presents its report thereon or in the following session.

A Demand for Excess Grant is made after the expenditure has actually been incurred and after the financial year to which it relates has expired. A Demand for Supplementary Grant, on the other hand, has necessarily to be presented and also passed during the financial year to which it relates. Demand for money already spent in excess of the voted Grant is made not by of Supplemeantary Demand but in the form of an Excess Grant.

Token Grants

Sometimes additional funds are not actually required to meet proposed expenditure on 'new services' on account of saving made under a sanctioned head which might be utilized for the 'new services' with the sanction of Parliament for such reappropriation. In such a case, a Demand for the grant of a token sum is submitted to the vote of the House. If the House assents to the Demand, funds are so made available. Token Grants generally form part of Supplementary Demands for Grants.

Votes of Credit

On account of some national emergency Government may require funds to meet an unexpected demand for money for which it may not be possible to give detailed estimates. In such a case, the House might grant the lump-sum money without details through a vote of credit passed by the House.

Exceptional Grants

An exceptional grant is made for a particular and special purpose which does not form part of the ordinary expenditure of the financial year. In that case, the House may separately grant funds for that special purpose.

Supplementary, additional, excess and exceptional grants and votes of credit are regulated by the same procedure as is applicable in the case of Demands for Grants, subject to such adaptations, whether by way of modification or omission, as the Speaker deems necessary or expedient. No demands for vote of credit or exceptional grant have so far been presented to Parliament.

The Appropriation Bill

The voting granted by Lok Sabha does not by itself authorise the issue of money out of the Consolidated Fund of India to meet the grants. The Constitution provides that no money shall be withdrawn from the Consolidated Fund of India except under appropriation made by law. The Appropriation Act is the only legal authority for the appropriation of money from the Consolidated Fund of India.

An Appropriation Bill provides for the appropriation out of the Consolidated Fund of India of money required to meet—

(a) The Grants made by Lok Sabha,
(b) The expenditure charged on the Consolidated Fund of India but not exceeding in any case the amount shown in the statement previously laid before Parliament.

The Bill is introduced in Lok Sabha after the Demands for Grants have been voted by Lok Sabha. Introduction of the Bill cannot be opposed.

An Appropriation Bill attracts the provisions of sub-clause (d) of Article 110(1) of the Constitution, namely, the appropriation of money out of the Consolidated Fund of India, and is certified by the Speaker as a Money Bill. It is introduced in, and considered by, Lok Sabha with the Presidents recommendation under Clauses (1) and (3) respectively of Article 117 of the Constitution. In Rajya Sabha the procedure is the same as in case of any other Money Bill.

The debate on the appropriation Bill is restricted to matters of public importance or administrative policy implied in the grants covered by the Bill which have not already been raised while the relevant Demands for Grants under discussion. The Speaker, in order to avoid repetition of debate, requires Members desiring to take part in discussion on an Appropriation Bill to give advance intimation of the specific points they intend to raise and he withholds permission for raising such of the points as in his opinion appear to be repetition of the matters discussed on a Demand for Grant or may not be of sufficient public importance.

In the case of an Appropriation Bill in pursuance of a Supplementary Grant in respect of an existing service, the discussion is confined to the items constituting the same and no discussion is raised on the original grant nor the policy underlying it except in so far as it may be necessary to explain or illustrate a particular item under discussion.

The Finance Bill

The Finance Bill is introduced in Lok Sabha immediately after the General Budget is presented to Lok Sabha by the Finance Minister.

The Finance Bill seeks to give effect to the financial proposals of the Govt. of India for the next (following) financial year. It also includes a Bill to give effect to supplementary financial proposal for any period.

The Finance Bill submits to the House all the Acts with which it deals e.g. the Income-Tax Act, Central Excise Act, etc. and the House can amend all or any of such Acts to the extent they are dealt with in the Finance Bill. The Speaker has held that the Finance Bill should not contain provisions intended to make permanent changes is existing laws unless they are consequential upon, or incidental to the taxation proposals.

There may be more than one Finance Bill during a year. In case a second Finance Bill containing supplementary taxation proposals is introduced, it has to be preceded by Demands for Grants and the connected Appropriation Bill; in other words, the sequence in regard to Budget as provided for in Articles 112 to 115 of the Constitution has got to be followed.

The provisions of the Finance Bill relating to imposition or increase in duties of customs and excise come into force immediately on the expiry of the day on which the Bill is introduced by virtue of a declaration under the Provisional Collection of Taxes Act, 1931, contained in the Bill, to the effect that it is expedient in the public interest that the provisions of certain clauses of the Bill shall have immediate effect. Such a provision has the force of law. The Finance Bill of 1957 and 1962 (election years) did not contain such a declaration.

A Finance Bill invariably attracts the provisions of sub-clause (a) of Article 110(1) of the Constitution, namely, the imposition, abolition, remission, alteration or regulation of any tax, and is certified by the Speaker as a Money Bill. It is introduced in Lok Sabha with President's recommendation under Articles 11(1) and 274(1) of the Constitution and is considered by Lok Sabha with the President's recommendation under Article 117(3). As in the case of an Appropriation Bill the procedure in Rajya Sabha in regard to Finance Bill is the same as in case of other Money Bills.

As the Finance Bill is a secret Bill, copies of the Bill are not circulated to Members before introduction. Copies of Bill are included in the sets of General Budget papers, which are made available to Members after the Budget is presented. Introduction of a Finance Bill cannot be opposed.

At any time after the introduction in the House of a Finance Bill, the Speaker may allot a day or days, jointly or serially, for the completing of all or any of the stages involved in the passage of the Bill by the House. In actual practice, however, the allocation of time is recommended by the Business Advisory Committee and is subsequently approved by the House. When such allotment of time has been made, the Speaker at 17.00 hrs. on the alloted day or on the last of the allotted days, as the case may be shall forthwith put all questions necessary to dispose of all the outstanding matters in connection with the stage or stages for which the day or days have been allotted. During the discussion on a Finance Bill, a Member can discuss matters relating to general administration, local grievances within the sphere of the responsibility of the Govt. of India, but actions of a State Government cannot be criticised in the discussion of a Finance Bill. While generally criticism of the policy of the government is permissible, discussion on details of particular estimates is not in order but a Member can discuss maters of public policy that contributed to a deficit. General principles underlying the Budget can be discussed but not the details of these principles. In short, the whole administration comes under review but questions which have already been discussed in a previous debate cannot be reopened.

Discussion on a clause of a Finance Bill and on amendments thereto has to be confined to the taxation proposed to possible alternatives.

The Finance Bill containing the annual taxation proposals is considered and passed by Lok Sabha only after the Demands for Grants have been voted and the total expenditure is known. There is, however, no statutory bar to considering a Bill containing permanent taxation measures before the Demands for Grants have been voted.

Budget of State under President's Rule

Budget of a State under President's Rule is presented to Lok Sabha. The procedure followed in regard to the Budget of the Central Government is followed in the case of State Budget also with such variations or modification, as the Speaker may make.

Thus, the Parliament in India controls all legislation and national finance, for and on behalf of the people of India. The Comptroller and Auditor-General acts as the 'watch-dog' of Parliament, and prepares reports on Ministries which form the basis for the working of the Public Accounts Committee. The Parliamentary financial control is very stringent and complete and it is the Lok Sabha which really exercises it. However, the Law-making power of the Indian Parliament is not as absolute as that in Great Britain because the Parliament here functions under a written Constitution and there is a difference between procedure of Law-Making and of Constitutional amendment. The Supreme Court has powers of judicial review over parliament legislation and executive orders.

4

COMMITTEE SYSTEM IN PARLIAMENT

The Committee system which has its origin in the British House of Commons has now come to stay in all legislatures including the Congress in the United States. Apart from giving an opportunity to deliberate in a more dispassionate and less partisan manner it also facilitates the close and sincere participation of those representatives of the people in a House who have a genuine interest, experience and at times expertise in the subject-matter of the Bill. A more business-like and down-to-earth approach is adopted and the functioning of the excutive Departments can be thoroughly screened. The report of a Committee forms the basis of discussions in the House which usually deliberates/thinks on Party lines. Much of the legislative business is thus handled through the Committees which are much smaller in size and represent all shades of opinions and views in Parliament *sans* the affront which often expressess itself in the House.

In Great Britain the Committees are: the Committee of the Whole House, Select Committees, Standing Committees of the House of Commons on Public Bills, Joint Committees of both Houses (Commons and Lords), Private Bill Committees.

In the United States of America the Committees are established and help the legislative process. While there are about sixteen Standing Committees in the Senate, the House of Representatives has twenty-two Committees. To site a few examples of powerful Committees from both these Houses it will be sufficient to name the Committees on Appropriation, Armed Services, Finance, Foreign Relations etc. from the Senate and the Committees on Appropriations, Armed Services, Budget, International Relations etc. from the House. There are some Special Committees in each House and Joint Committees of both Houses. It is through a Joint Committee of both Houses that efforts are made to resolve the differences between the two Houses on Bills, failing which the Bill's consideration is given up.

Committees in Indian Parliament

Following the British tradition we have an elaborate committee system, both in Lok Sabha and Rajya Sabha. Each Committee is constituted in such manner that it represents a replica of the House in miniature. The Members of these Committees enjoy the same rights and powers/ privileges in respect of freedom of speech, arrest etc. as are enjoyed by Members of the House. A Parliamentary Committee is either appointed/elected by the House or nominated by the Speaker. It gets full Secretarial support. They may be either Standing Committees which are elected or nominated every year are from time to time, and to that extent may be considered as permanent, or they may be *ad hoc* Committees which are meant for a particular purpose or function and become defunct as soon as their work is over. These also may be elected by the House or nominated by the Speaker.

The following Committees are elected by the Lok Sabha every year. These are :

Standing Committees

(i) Committee on Public Accounts,
(ii) Estimates Committee,
(iii) Committee on Public Undertakings,
(The above three are Financial Committees)
(iv) Committee on the Welfare of Scheduled Castes and Scheduled Tribes.

In the case of the first and the third and fourth of the above Committees, Members of Rajya Sabha also elect their Members on the Committees.

The Joint Committee on Offices of Profit is also a Standing Committee elected by the Lok Sabha.

All other Standing Committees are nominated by the Speaker. These include :

(i) The Business Advisory Committee,
(ii) The Rules Committee,
(iii) The Privileges committee,
(iv) The Petitions Committee,

(v) The Committee on Government Assurances,
(vi) The Committee on Private Members' Bills and Resolutions,
(vii) The Committee on Absence of Members from the Sittings of the House,
(viii) Library Committee,
(ix) House Committee,
(x) General Purposes Committee,
(xi) Committee on Sub-ordinate Legislation,
(xii) Committee on Papers laid on the Table, and
(xiii) Joint Committee on Salaries and Allowances of Members of Parliament.

Ad hoc Committees

These committees which are for a particular purpose or function and only for that time-span may be appointed by the House or by the Speaker either by himself or on the recommendations of a Parliamentary Committee. Examples are: Five Year Plan Committees, Committees appointed on the Conduct of Members, for Amendment of Election Law (1970), Committee on the Use of Language etc.

Select or Joint Committees on Bills are also *ad hoc* Committees and are examples of Committees appointed by the House. Usually a Motion for reference to a Select Committee also specifics the names of Members for the Committee. In case of Government Bill the Minister in charge of the Bill is appointed as Member of the Committee.

The Speaker appoints Chairmen of all Standing Committees.

In case of the Committee on Public Accounts, the Membership is in proportion to different parties and groups in the House so that they are represented in proportion to their respective strength in the House. As per a well-settled British Convention, the Chairman of the Committee on Public Accounts ought to be from the main opposition parties or groups and in a rotating manner. However, this convention has not been established or strictly followed in India.

In Indian Parliament there is no Committee of the Whole House and the Mace on the table of the Speaker (much relevant for the said Committee) is also absent.

Details about some important Committees are given below:

Select or Joint Committees

These Committees may be appointed at the first stage of the Second Reading of the Bill in the House. The Member-in-charge of the Bill may himself move the Bill to refer it to a Select Committee of the House, or any other Member may also move the matter by suggesting an amendment to refer it to a Select Committee. The Bill may be referred to a Joint Committee, with the concurrence of the Rajya Sabha, composed of members of both the Houses.

Though the motion suggesting reference to a Select Committee suggests the names of Members, additional Members may be appointed on the suggestion of the member-in-charge and adopted by the House. The number of members is not fixed but usually it varies between 30 to 35 . The Members must give consent for working on the committee. The Minister-in-charge of a Bill is always appointed as Member. Even when a Minister is not a Member on the Committee but wants to participate, is allowed to do so but is not allowed to vote. Experts who are not Members may be called as witnesses but they don't participate in the deliberation. The Committee may even hear representatives of special interests affected by the measure. Its sitting may be held within the precincts of Parliament House with the prior permission of Speaker or outside for hearing oral evidence. The Committee may visit places in the country or even visit a foreign country for on-the-spot studies.

These committees may amend or revise the Bill but these alterations must be within the scope of the Bill and not against the principle of the Bill. It may re-draft the Bill, insert provisions or restrict the scope. For taxation proposals, prior recommendation of the President must be obtained before such changes/restrictions etc. The Legislative Counsel from the Legislative Department of the Ministry of Law, Justice and Company Affairs who attends meetings gets the amendments incorporated in the Bill.

If no specific time-limit is fixed by the House for the Committee to submit its report, it must do so before the expiry of three months from the date of passing the motion creating the Committee in the House. The Draft Report is submitted to its Chairman for his approval and also to the Legislative Counsil. Later, the Report is presented to the Lok Sabha and in case of a Joint Committee, simultaneously to the Rajya Sabha. With the presentation of the report the Committee ceases to function i.e. becomes *functus officio.*

Committee of Privileges

After a new House is constituted after elections, the Speaker nominates a Committee of Privileges consisting of not more than 15 members. The Chairman of the Committee is also appointed by the Speaker from among the Members of the Committee. Though no fixed term of office has been specified, it is appointed each year along with other Committees. As and when the Deputy Speaker is a Member of the Privileges Committee, he is appointed as its Chairman. On all procedural matters at the sittings, Chairman's decision is final and in case of doubt he may refer the point to the Speaker whose decision is final. The Speaker can give directions to the Committee in connection with matters connected with Privileges.

The Committee examines and decides all matters concerned with Privileges referred to it. It can hear the concerned Member(s) of the House, and listens to oral or written evidence. Witnesses may be summoned to appear before it. The report of the Committee is presented to the House and a resolution is moved by its Chairman to seek approval of the House. If it is adopted the Speaker implements the decision. If the Lok Sabha is dissolved, the questions of privileges pending before the Committee automatically lapse.

The Business Advisory Committee

The Committee consists of not more than 15 Members nominated by the Speaker. Though he tries to make it broad-based, he also invites members from different groups to attend the meetings, though not as Members. The Speaker is *ex-officio* Chairman of the Committee. The main function of the Committee is to allot time in respect of Government bills and other business including Private Members. The time order is fixed and changes are not allowed except on a motion made with the consent of the Speaker and accepted by the House.

The Financial Committees

Under the Indian Constitution no money can be drawn or spent by Central Government out of state coffers except under the authority of law passed by Parliament. Parliament alone has the power of the purse. Government proposals for expenditure out of the Consolidated Fund of India are presented to Lok Sabha in the form of Demands for Grants at the commencement of each Financial Year and also if necessary, as Supplementary Demands for grants during the course of the year. These are discussed and voted by Lok Sabha before the law authorising the Government to draw and spend the moneys is passed by Parliament. The Parliamentary control over public expenditure is, however, not limited only to the voting of moneys required by Government for carrying on the administration of the country but also extends to ensuring that expenditure is incurred in a prudent manner on plans and programmes approved by Parliament and that the objectives underlying the plans and programmes are achieved. Even though Lok Sabha discusses the Demands for Grants for sufficiently long period before voting, due to magnitude and complexity of the state activities, it is almost impossible for Parliament as a body to scrutinise the myriad of expenditure proposals and government activities effectively or minutely. In fact, it has neither the time for a thorough scrutiny of the plethora of items included in the Demands for Grants or achievements claimed by Government nor, because of its size and procedures, is it suited for such a task.

In order to help it exercise effective control over public expenditure, Lok Sabha has set up three Financial Committees viz. Public Accounts Committee, Estimates Committee and Committee on Public Undertakings. (Besides these three committees Railway Convention Committee an *ad hoc* Committee, when set up, functions like a Financial Committee.) While the Public Accounts Committee and the Estimates Committee deal with the Ministeries and Departments of Government and statutory bodies under their control, the Public Undertaking Committee directs its attention to working of public undertakings of the Central Government.

These Committees keep an unremitting vigil over governmental spending and performance, bring to light inefficiencies, waste and indiscretion in the implemention of policies and programmes approved by Parliament and make recommendations to tone up the administration for economic, efficient and speedy execution of these policies and programmes. The relentless crusade of the Financial Committees to this and keeps the administration on its toes and secures its accountability to Parliament. These Committees also provide a forum for interaction between Government Departments and Parliament and a medium for information and ideas to follow in both directions.

Composition

While Estimates Committee is a Committee consisting of 30 members exclusively from the Lok Sabha, the other two Committees are in the nature of Joint Committees of Parliament, in that they consist of members of both the Houses of Parliament, 15 from Lok Sabha 7 from Rajya Sabha. The members are elected every year from amongst the members of the respective Houses according to principle of proportional representation by means of single transferable vote.

This system of election ensures the representation of almost all parties and groups in Parliament, more or less, in proportion to their strength in the Houses. Ministers are debarred from becoming members of these committees. If a member elected to any of these Committees is subsequently appointed Minister, he ceases to be a member of the Committees. It is thus ensured that these Committees function absolutely independent of the influence of the Ministers and bring to bear an objective approach to the matters under scrutiny.

Appointment of Chairmen

The Chairmen of these Committees are appointed by the Speaker from amongst the Members of the Committee.

Since 1967, by convention, the Chairman has been a leading Member of the opposition party or Group. Since inception the Chairman of the Committee of Public Undertakings has been a senior member of the Committee from the ruling party except during the period 1977-79 when a Member of an opposition Group was appointed its Chairman. The Chairman of the Estimates Committee has always been a senior Member from the ruling party.

Term of Office

These committees are elected for a term not exceeding on year.

According to a convention observed by some of the national political parties, their members are allowed a two-year term on the Committee. This is done by renomination of a member of the outgoing Committee for election to the succeeding Committee.

Non-Party Character

The Committees have functioned in a non-party spirit and their deliberations and conclusions have been objective and this in a large measure accounts for the respect in which their recommendations are held. They have acquired a reputation of working in an atmosphere of complete cordiality in which the various shades of opinion represented on the committee try to find out the maximum area of agreement.

Powers

The committees have powers to frame their own rules of internal working with the approval of the Speaker. The powers, privileges and immunities of these committees and their members are the same as those of the House. They have, in particular, the power to send for persons, papers or records and except where production of a document is certified by Government to be prejudicial to the safety or interest of the state, refusal to appear before the committees or produce any document demanded by them may tantamount to breach of privilege and contempt of the committee.

The Public Accounts Committee

Functions

The Committee examines the accounts showing the appropriation of sums granted by the House for the expenditure of Government of India, the annual finance accounts of the Government of India and such other accounts laid before the House as the Committee may think fit. Since the year 1962-63 the Committee has also started examining the revenue receipts of the Government of India. If any money has been spent by the Government on any service during the financial year in excess of the amount granted by the House for that purpose, the Committee examines with reference to the facts of each case the circumstances leading to such an excess and presents a report thereon the House.

The Committee does not exercise its functions in relation to such Public Undertaking as are allotted to the Public Undertakings Committee under the Rules of Procedure of Lok Sabha or by the Speaker.

The functions of the Committee extend beyond formality of expenditure, to the wisdom, faithfulness and economy of such expenditure.

Bases for Selection of Items

Public Accounts Committee

The time and attention of the Public Accounts Committee is mainly devoted to the examination and consideration of appropriation accounts and the Audit Reports of the Comptroller and Auditor-General of India thereon. However, in the past the Committee have also inquired into the various irregularities which have become public or which have been brought to the notice of the Government even through no formal audit report has been presented on the subject.

The Audit Reports presented by the C & A.G. to the President, upon being laid on the Table of the House, stand referred to the Committee. These reports are scrutinised by the Committee and the Paragraphs in these reports are categorised into: (a) Most Important, (b) Important, and (c) Not so important. In the case of paragraphs of the audit reports categorised as 'Most Important', oral evidence of the representatives of the Ministries/Deptts. etc. concerned is taken before the Committee reports to the House. The Committee's Reports on paragraphs categorised as 'Important' are based on written information obtained from the Government.

Information from Government

The Public Accounts Committee gets from the Comptroller and Auditor-General of India the Memoranda of Important Points (MIP) on the paragraphs selected by the Committee for examination which are categorised as 'Most Important" or 'Important'. On basis of the MIP a list of points is drawn up and sent to the Ministry/Department concerned for furnishing information by a prescribed date. The list of points on paragraphs categorised as 'most important', however, contains points calling for statistical data or detailed information which cannot be given by the representatives of the Ministry during oral evidence. This data and information has to be furnished to the Committee well before the oral evidence of the representatives of the Ministry so that it could be used by members during oral evidence. Based on the information furnished by the Government to the Committee, a further list of points may be drawn up for obtaining detailed information from the Government in writing.

The Estimates Committee

The function of this Committee is to report on the economies, improvements in organisation, efficiency or administrative reform which may be effected by Ministries/Departments of the Central Government or statutory and other Government bodies under their control, consistent with the Policy underlying the estimates. The Committee can suggest alternative policies in order to bring about efficiency and economy in administration. The Committee also examines whether the money is well laid out within the limits of the policy implied in the estimates.

The Committee does not exercise its functions in relation to such Public Undertakings as are allotted to the Public Undertaking Committee by the Rules of Procedure of Lok Sabha or by the Speaker.

The Committee may also examine matters of special interest, which though unconnected with the estimates of any particular Ministry/Department of the Government may arise or come to light in the course of its work which it may consider necessary to bring to the notice of the House.

The Committee continues the examination of the estimates from time to time throughout the financial year and may report to the House as its examination proceeds or on the conclusion of the examination.

Selection of Subjects

At the beginning of its term every year, the Committee selects subjects concerning the estimates of a Ministry/Department of Central Government or such statutory and Government organisations subordinate thereto, as do not fall within the purview of the Committee on Public Undertakings, for examination during the year.

Obtaining Information from Government

After the subjects are selected by the Committee for examination, the Departments/Ministries are asked to furnish preliminary information on the subjects within a specified time. For this purpose, a Questionnaire on each subject is drawn up and supplied to the Ministry/ Department concerned. After going through the Preliminary material, the Members may suggest points on which further information is required by them. All the important points emerging as a result of an independent study of the preliminary material and other literature on a subject, including the points suggested by the members, are consolidated in the form of a questionnaire and after approval by the Study Group/Chairman, the questionnaire is sent to the concerned Ministries/Departments for reply in writing.

Committee on Public Undertakings

As in the case of Estimates Committee, the Committee on Public Undertakings at the beginning of its term selects a few Undertakings or any of their activities for examination and report. The Committee may also take up horizontal study of any subject involving all the Public Undertakings. Some of the Undertakings selected for examination are those for which appraisals appear in the Audit Report (Commercial) of the C & AG and some Undertakings are selected by the Committee for independent examination on its own.

As soon as the Committees are constituted, each Committee is divided into several working/study groups. These groups area appointed by the Chairman of the Committee.

Each of the Study/Working Groups is headed by the Convener. The function of a Working/Study Group is to make a detailed study of the audit Paragraphs (in the case of Public Accounts Committee) or subjects assigned to the group and to generally assist the committee in the exemination of such Audit Paragraphs/subjects. The system of Working/Study Groups enables the Members to apply themselves intensively to the study of subjects according to their aptitudes and also encourages specialization among Members. The Working/Study Groups do not take oral evidence, nor do they draw a report.

When however the Estimates Committee selects for examination any part of the estimates of the Ministry of Defence, it appoints a Sub-Committee on Defence for examining the estimates of that Ministry.

Unlike the Study Groups, the Sub-Committee on Defence, like any other Sub-Committee has adequate powers, of which the most notable are the powers to take oral evidence and to draw up a report which is deemed to be a report of the whole Committee if approved by the latter. The Committee examines the reports and Accounts of the Public Undertakings specified in the Rules of Procedure including the report of the Camptroller and Auditor General thereon. It is the function of the Committee to see whether the affairs of the Public Undertakings are being managed in accordance with sound business principles and prudent commercial practices or not. The Committee is precluded from examining: (i) matters of major Government policy (ii) matters of day-to-day administration; and (iii) matters for the consideration of which a statutory machinery already exists.

Where the Committee undertakes an examination of the Public Undertakings or any aspect of the working of the Public Undertakings on the basis of an appraisal contained in the Audit report of the C & AG, the procedure for calling for information from the Government is the same as in the case of examination of audit paragraphs by the Public Accounts Committee. In cases where an undertaking or a subject pertaining thereto has been taken up for examination by the Committee on its own, the procedure for calling information from the Government is same as in the case of Estimates Committee, namely, in the first instance preliminary material is called for and later, on the basis of a study of the information furnished by the Government and independent studies, a detailed questionnaire is drawn up and addressed to the

Ministers/Public Undertakings concerned to furnish detailed information on the undertakings/subjects.

Memoranda from Non-Officials

The Estimates Committee and the Committee on Public Undertakings have the system of calling memoranda on the subjects/Undertakings selected by them for examination, from leading non-official organisation like Chambers of Commerce and Industry, Trade Associations,, Professional Bodies, Institutes of Management, Professional Consultants and eminent individuals having special expertise or knowledge of the subjects which could be of advantage and use to the committees in their examination. The Committee on Public Undertakings, in addition and where considered necessary, calls for memoranda also from companies in the private sector and from chief office bearers of registered Trade Unions of the Public Undertakings under examination. For this purpose questionnaires on each subject are drawn up and forwarded to the organisations/ individuals for furnishing memoranda by a specified date.

The Public Accounts Committee does not have such a system. The examination of audit paragraphs by the committee is based on the assistance provided by the C & AG and his organisation and the written or/and oral evidence of the Ministries/Departments concerned.

Study Tours

The Financial Committees undertake tours, with the approval of the Speaker, for an on-the-spot study of the working of local offices, establishments or undertakings under examination. For this purpose the Committee is divided into two to three groups, each headed by a Convener. During the tour the Group may also hold informal discussion with local officers, project authorities, head of establishment/ undertaking or where necessary, with the representatives of concerned non-official organisations located at the place of visit. The informal discussion is only to elicit information relevant to the matter under examination and to have a general idea of the working of the local office/institution/undertaking and further to know first hand the local problems and views on matters under examination. No decisions are taken at these informal discussions nor any evidence recorded. A note summing up the impressions of the Group and salient points raised during the informal discussions with officers and others during the tour is prepared and circulated to all the Members of the Committee.

Further information, if any, required by the Committee in the light of the impressions gained during the tours is obtained from the Ministry/ Department concerned.

Evidence of Non-Officials

After the memoranda from non-officials are received these are studied. Where considered necessary, selected non-official organisations individuals are invited to appear before the committee to tender evidence. When it is decided to hear a non-official he is invited to appear before the Committee on a specified date and time. For this purpose, a list of points for oral evidence is drawn up and supplied to the witness in advance of the evidence.

This system of calling Memoranda from, and taking oral evidence of, non-officials enables the Committee to know the views of knowledgeable persons reflecting public interest on the subject under examination and places at the disposal of the Committee useful data and information which can be tested out during oral examination of the representatives of the Ministries/Undertakings

As stated earlier the Public Accounts Committee does not have the system of either calling memoranda from non-officials or inviting any of them for oral evidence.

Evidence of Officials

Public Accounts Committee

After the study of the Memoranda of important points furnished by the Comptroller and Auditor-General and written information obtained in advance from the Ministry concerned and tour notes, a list of points is drawn up for oral evidence of the representatives of the Ministry concerned.

Estimates Committee

The list of points for oral evidence of the representatives of the Ministry concerned with the subject under examination is drawn after a study of the preliminary material, written information received from the Ministry to questionnaires addressed to them, tour notes, memoranda from non-officials and oral evidence of non-officials.

Committee on Public Undertakings

The Committee has developed a convention whereby the representatives of a public undertaking are examined separately from the administrative Ministry/Department concerned. This is done with a view to afford to the undertaking an opportunity to put forward its point of view freely and frankly. The evidence of the representatives of the administrative Ministry concerned is based on the lists of points drawn up after intensive study of the material and evidence collected by the Committee from various sources.

Post-Evidence Replies

There may be certain points on which the witnesses are unable to furnish information to the committee during evidence itself. In such cases the Chairman may permit the witness to furnish the reply subsequently in writing. It may also well be that all the points on which discussion is proposed to be held are not covered during evidence for paucity of time. All such points are consolidated and the list of points arising out of evidence is sent to the Ministry concerned for furnishing replies in writing within a specified time.

Report

On the basis of the preliminary material and detailed information obtained from the Ministry/Undertaking in writing tour notes, memoranda from non-officials, verbatim record of proceedings of the Committee containing evidence of non-officials and officials, and written information obtained from the Ministry on points arising out of evidence, the Committee finalise their Reports. The Report on a subject is divided into chapters, sections and paragraphs dealing with different aspects of working of the Ministry/Undertaking examined by the Committee. The narrative portion summarizes the authenticated information obtained from the Ministry and other sources and the non-official and official view point on the subject expressed during evidence followed by observations and/or recommendations of the committee. After the draft Report is got factually verified from the ministry concerned (in the case of PAC reports and Audit-based reports of Committee on Public Undertakings from the C&AG), it is presented to the House by the Chairman of the Committee. In the case of PAC and PUC, a copy of the report is simultaneously laid on the Table of Rajya Sabha also.

Follow-Up of Reports

Parliamentary procedure in Lok Sabha envisages an elaborate system of follow-up of the recommendations made in the Reports of the Financial Committees. After presentation of the Reports, copies of Reports are forwarded to the Ministries/Departments/Undertakings concerned for taking action on the recommendations made therein. The Ministry/Department concerned with the Report are required to furnish to Lok Sabha Secretariat a statement showing the action taken by them on the recommendations contained in the Report within six months from the date of presentation of the Report except in cases where the committee may have desired the action taken to be reported to the Committee earlier.

The replies of the Government to the recommendations contained in the Reports of the Public Accounts Committee (PAC) and Audit-based Reports of the Committee on Public Undertakings (PUCs.) are required to be vetted by the Comptroller and Auditer-General of India before being furnished to the Committee.

The statement showing the action taken by Government is considered by the concerned Study Group/Action Taken Sub-Committee of the Committee concerned. The replies of the Government and the recommendations of the Study Group/Sub-Committee/ Committee are placed before the Chairman. The Draft Reports are presented to the House.

Action on Action Taken Reports

After an Action Taken Report is presented to the House, copies are sent to the Ministries/Undertakings concerned for action. Where a Ministry concerned is asked to furnish final replies in respect of recommendations contained in Chapter V of the Action Taken Report or any information or latest position in respect of recommendations reiterated or referred to in Chapter I and II thereof, the final replies, information or the latest position, as the case may be, has to be furnished to the Committee by a specified date, or in the absence thereof, within six months of the presentation of the Action Taken Report.

Replies or communications received in pursuance of the recommendations contained in the Action Taken Reports are laid on the Table of the House.

Railway Convention Committee

The Railway Convention Committee is an *ad hoc* Committee constituted from time to time to review the rate of dividend which is payable by the Railway undertaking to the general revenues as well as other ancillary matters in connection with railway finance vis-a-vis general finance and make recommendations thereon.

By a Resolution adopted in September 1924, the Legislative Assembly approved what is commonly known as the 'separation convention' providing for a definite annual contribution from the Railways to the General Revenues which was to be the first charge on the net receipt of the Railways. The working of the separation convention was reviewed from time to time by Committees appointed by the Legislative Assembly. The Railway Convention Committee 1949 was the first to be set up after Independence.

While the Railway Convention Committees of 1949, 1954, 1960, and 1965 confined themselves only to the question of determining the rate of dividend payable by Railways during the succeeding quinquennium, the Railway Convention Committee 1971 for the first time selected some subjects for detailed examination and presented reports to parliament covering not only the question of dividend but also diverse subjects pertaining to Railways' working. The Committee's of 1973, 1977, and 1980 followed suit.

The Committee consists of 18 members, 12 from Lok Sabha and 6 from Rajya Sabha appointed by the presiding officers of the respective houses. The Ministers of Finance and Railways are among the members of the Committee.

Although the Committee has not drawn up any separate rules to regulate its internal working, its procedure of work is the same as that of the Estimates Committee.

A New Era in Committee System

During the Budget session of the Indian Parliament i.e. during February 1993, a major break-through was effected so as to establish a closer and more effective control on finances by the Parliament. In 1979 such a control through Committees was established in Great Britain. India's Vice-President Shri K.R. Narayanan, welcoming this change, said that the new Committees would ensure efficiency of Parliamentary control over finances and a better answerability of the Executive to the Parliament:

These new Standing Committees started functioning in April

1993. In all seventeen Standing Committees were established. Three committees were for the Ministries of Home, Defence and Foreign Affairs respectively and the remaining fourteen covered the remaining Ministries/Departments. These Committees would examine thoroughly the Demands for Grants of all Ministries/Departments and submit reports to both Houses. They would also examine all important Bills and Policy matters sent to them and submit compact reports (not exceeding 20 pages) to the House.

Membership of each Committee would be 45, out of which 30 Members should be from the Lok Sabha and 15 Members from the Rajya Sabha. While Chairmen of six Committees would be from the Rajya Sabha, Chairmen of eleven Committees should be from the Lok Sabha. Out of the above six, Chairmen of three committees should go to the main opposition parties in Parliament. Shri Shivraj Patil, Speaker said that even the smallest party in the Parliament should get the opportunity of heading one of these Committees.

These new Committees would function *in addition* to the already existing Committees of the House(s) and would not affect their importance or functioning. Ministers, Secretaries of the concerned Ministries/Departments could be asked to appear before these Committees and supply imformation as well as answer queries. The work would be done dispassionately, crossing party lines and in a business-like manner. All these Committees would submit their reports to the House(s) where they may be discussed and final decisions arrived at. A fear has been expressed that those Members from both Houses who may not be on any of these Committees might be marginalised. However as the House(s) would be discussing the Committee reports, this fear seems to be unfounded.

5

PRIVILEGES OF THE PARLIAMENT

Privileges—Meaning

What is a Privilege

Privilege is an exceptional right or exemption. It means an exemption from some duty, burden, attendance or liability to which others are subject. In a Parliamentary system it indicates rights and immunities enjoyed by each House of Parliament collectively, and by members of each House individually but for which they cannot discharge their functions. The purpose is to safeguard the freedom and the dignity of Parliament. The proper exercise of the functions entrusted to Parliament by the Constitution will be impossible without them.

Privileges are granted to members to perform their duty in Parliament without any fear or hindrance. They are related only to the performance in the House and its functions. Thereby the members are not absolved of the obligations to the society nor do these privileges place them on a footing different from that of an ordinary citizen.

The privilege against assault or molestation is applicable only when a member is obstructed or molested while discharging his duties as a Member of Parliament. A libel or a reflection upon a Member of Parliament which does not concern his character or conduct in his capacity as a Member of the House or is not based on matters arising in the actual transaction of the business of the House does not affect his privilege. There are no exemptions from the operation of the ordinary laws of the land. Thus while legislators returning from session of the House were ill treated by Railway staff on Railway Station it was considered as a breach of privilege.

Members' Privileges Under the Constitution

(i) Freedom of Speech in Parliament, and

(ii) Immunity of Members from any proceedings in Courts in respect of any thing said or any vote given by them in Parliament.

[Articles 105 (1), (2)]

Prior to Section 15 of the Constitution (44th Amendment) Act, 1978 which came into force with effect from 20th June 1979, Article 105 provided that the power privileges "shall be those of the House of Commons of the Parliament of the United Kingdom, and of its members and committees at the commencement of the Constitution, i.e. on the 26th January 1950." After the said Amendment, the powers and privileges are based on the precedents and conventions which have grown in this country, in terms of the provisions of the Constitution [Article 105 (3)] .

The purpose of the Amendment to Article 105(3), made in June 1979, was that the original provision (and there was no escape from it) had referred to the British House of Commons. A proud country like India would like to avoid making any reference to a foreign institution in its own solemn constitutional document. Therefore, this verbal change was introduced by this clause so that there may not be any reference to a foreign institution.

However, as no law under Article 105/194 is yet enacted, the powers, privileges and immunities of the Houses of Parliament and state legislatures and of the Members and the Committees of the House continue to be governed by the precedents of the British House of Commons as they existed on the date our Constitution came into force. Thus the change is more verbal than being actual.

Article 105 of the Constitution reads as follows:

"(1) Subject to the provisions of this Constitution and to the rules and standing orders regulating the procedure of Parliament, there shall be freedom of Speech in Parliament.

(2) No Member of Parliament shall be liable to any proceedings in any Court in respect of anything said or any vote given by him in Parliament or any Committee thereof, and no person shall be so liable in respect of the publication by or under the authority of either House of Parliament of any report, paper, votes or proceedings.

(3) In other respects, the powers, privileges and immunities of each House of Parliament, and of the members and the Committees of each House, shall be such as may from time to time be defined by Parliament by law, and, until, so defined,

shall be those of that House and of its members and Committees immediately before the coming into force of Section 15 of the Constitution. (Forty-Fourth Amendment) Act, 1978.

(4) The provisions of clauses (1), (2) and (3) shall apply in relation to persons, who by virtue of this Constitution have the right to speak in, and otherwise to take part in the proceedings of a House of Parliament or any committee thereof as they apply in relation to Members of Parliament".

Article 194 of the Constitution contains the corresponding provisions relating to the powers, privileges and immunities of the Houses of State Legislatures which are similar to those in Article 105 relating to Parliament.

It has been urged that codification of the law of privileges is urgent and essential so as to make the position clear and free from ambiguity. On the contrary it is also opined that any codification is more likely, to harm the prestige and sovereignty of Parliament, State Legislatures without any benefit being conferred on the Press and that in the present circumstances, codification of Parliamentary Privileges is neither necessary nor desirable.

Former Chief Justice of India and former Vice-President of India and Chairman, Rajya Sabha, Mr.J. Hiadayatullah said:

> "If there is mutual trust and respect between Parliament and Courts there is hardly any need to codify law on the subject of Privileges. With a codified law more advantage will flow to persons bent on vilifying Parliament, its members and Committees and the Courts will be called upon more and more to intervene. At the moment, given a proper understanding on both sides, Parliamentary right to punish for breach of its privileges and contempt would rather receive the support of Courts than otherwise. A written law will make in difficult for Parliament as well as Courts to maintain that dignity which rightly belongs to Parliament and which the Courts will always uphold as zealously as they uphold their own."

Important Privileges of each House of Parliament

(1) Freedom of speech in Parliament (Article 105(1) of the Constitution).

(2) Immunity to a member from any proceedings in any Court in

respect of any thing said or any vote given by him in Parliament or any of its Committee (Article 105(2) of the Constitution).

(3) Immunity to a persons from proceedings in any court in respect of the publication by or under the authority of either House of Parliament of any report, paper, votes or proceedings (Article 105(2) of the Constitution).

(4) Prohibition on the Courts to inquire into proceedings of Parliament (Article 122 of the Constitution).

(5) Freedom from arrest of members in Civil cases during the continuance of the session of the House and forty days before its commencement and forty days after its conclusion (Section 135(A) of the Code of Civil Procedure).

(6) Exemption of members from liability to serve as Juror.

(7) Right of the House to receive immediate information of the arrest, detention, conviction, imprisonment and release of a member.

(8) Prohibition of arrest and service of legal process within the precincts of the House without obtaining the permission of the Speaker.

(9) Prohibition of disclosure of the proceedings or decisions of a secret sitting of the House.

(10) Members or Officers of the House cannot give evidence or produce documents in Courts of law, relating to the proceedings of the House without the permission of the House.

(11) Members or Officers of the House cannot attend as a witness before the other house or a Committee thereof or before a House of State Legislature or a Committee thereof without the permission of the House and they cannot be compelled to do so without their consent.

(12) All Parliamentary Committees are empowered to send for persons, papers, and records relevant for the purpose of the inquiry by a committee. A witness may be required to produce such documents as are required for the use of a committee.

(13) A Parliamentary Committee may administer oath or affirmation to a witness examined before it.

(14) The evidence tendered before a parliamentary committee and its report and proceedings cannot be disclosed or published by anyone until these have been laid on Table of the House.

Powers of each House

(i) to commit persons, whether they are members or not, for breach of privilege or contempt of the House,

(ii) to compel the attendance of witnesses and to send for papers and records,
(iii) to regulate its own procedure and the conduct of its business (Article 118 of the Constitution),
(iv) to prohibit the publication of its debates and proceedings, and
(v) to exclude strangers from the House.

Breach of Privilege

Disregard or attack on any of the Privileges, rights and immunities of the members individually or of the House is an offence and is called a breach of privilege and is punishable by the House. Similarly, disobedience to its authority, its members or officers, is also punishable as contempt of the House.

Any act or omission which obstructs or impedes either House of Parliament in the performance of its functions, or which obstructs or impedes any member or officer of such house in the discharge of his duty, or which has tendency, directly or indirectly, to produce such results is considered as a contempt of Parliament.

Some Acts amounting to the Contempt of Parliament

(i) Speeches or writings reflecting on the House, its committees or members;
(ii) Reflections on the character and impartiality of the Speaker in the discharge of his duty;
(iii) Publication of false or distorted report of the proceedings of the House;
(iv) Publication of expunged proceedings of the House;
(v) Publication of proceedings of secret sessions of the House;
(vi) Premature publication of proceedings, evidence of report of a Parliamentary Committee;
(vii) Reflections on the report of Parliamentary Committee;
(viii) Molestation of members on account of their conduct in the House or obstructing members while in the performance of their duties as members or while on their way to or from, attending the House or a Committee thereof;
(ix) Offering bribes to members to influence them in their parliamentary conduct;
(x) Intimidation of members in connection with their Parliamentary conduct;
(xi) Obstructing or molesting officers of the House in the execution

of their duties;

(xii) Giving false or misleading evidence or information dileberately to the House or a Committee thereof, by a member or a witness; and

(xiii) Obstructing or molesting any witness during his attendance in the House or evidence as such witness before the House or a Committee thereof.

Power of Parliament to Punish for Contempt

House is the guardian of its privileges and the Courts of Law have recognised it. A person found quilty of breach or privilege or contempt of the House can either be reprimanded or admonitioned or be punished with imprisonment. In case of its own Members, suspension from the service of the House and expulsion is also possible.

Power to punish extends for contempts committed by members or by persons who are not members, irrespective of weather the offence is committed within the House or beyond it.

Punishments for Contempt of the House

Imprisonment

The period is limited by the duration of the session of the House. As soon as the House is prorogued, the prisoner is set at liberty.

Admonition or Reprimand

Admonition is the mildest form of punishment, and reprimand is the more serious form of displeasure of the House. Editor of *Blitz* was reprimanded for publishing libellous despatch in his magazine.

There are two other punishments for its Members :

(i) Suspension from the service of the House, and
(ii) Expulsion from the House.

The Select Committee on Parliamentary Privileges of House of Commons (U.K.) 1967 made the following recommendations :

"The House should exercise its penal jurisdiction: (a) in any event as sparingly as possible, and (b) only when it is satisfied that to do so is essential in order to provide reasonable protection for the House, its Members or its officers from such improper obstruction or attempt at or threat of obstruction as is causing, is likely to cause, substantial interference with the performance of their respective functions."

The Committee of Privileges of the House of Commons in their Third Report (1976-77) reiterated this recommendation and the House of Commons, U.K. adopted it on 6 February 1978.

The Committee of Privileges of 7th Lok Sabha in their First Report presented to the House on 8 May, 1981, observed *inter alia* as follows:

> "The Committee feel that it adds to the dignity of one and all if power in a democratic system is exercised with restraint; the more powerful a body or institution is, the greater restraint is called for particularly in exercising its penal jurisdiction".

Unqualified and unconditional regrets sincerely expressed by the persons guilty of breach of privilege and contempt of the House are accepted.

Freedom of Speech

It is the most important privilege embodied in clauses (1) and (2) of Article 105 of the Constitution originating from Article 9 of the Bill of Rights, 1689 of the United Kingdom which mentions :

> "That the freedom of speech, and debate or proceedings in Parliament, ought not to be impeached or questioned in any Court or place out of Parliament".

The Committee of Privileges Observed

> "It would be impeding a Member of Parliament in the discharge of his duties as such Member if he is to be questioned in any place outside Parliament for a disclosure that he may make in Parliament. The right of a Member of Parliament to function freely and without fear or favour is in India, as in the U.K., a constitutional guarantee. This guarantee is subject only to the rules of the House and ultimately to the disciplinary jurisdiction of the House itself . . . any investigation outside Parliament of anything that a Member says or does in the discharge of his

duties as a Member of Parliament would amount to a serious interference within the Member's right to carry out his duties as such Member."

Restriction on Freedom

In our Constitution, Article 121 provides that the conduct of any judge of the Supreme Court or of a High Court in the discharge of his duties shall not be discussed in Parliament except upon a motion for presenting an address to the President praying for the removal of the judge. Making of unwarranted allegations against a person is not allowed. In such cases the Speaker may direct him to discontinue his speech, or order the defamatory, indecent or unparliamentary or undignified words used by the Member to be expunged from the proceedings of the House. He may direct the Member to quit the House, or may put the question of suspension of the Member from the House to the vote of the House.

Though the words uttered by Members in the House may be false and malicious too and though a speech delivered by a Member in the House may amount to contempt of Court, no action can be taken against him in a Court of Law. Even the Official Secrets Act cannot be applied to the Member's speech in the House.

However, criminal acts committed by Members within the house cannot be regarded as a part of the proceedings of the House, for purposes of protection.

A breach of privilege and contempt of House is committed if someone obstructs or molests member while in the execution of his duties, while he is attending the house or when he is coming to, or going from, the House. Such acts committed against members have always been deemed to be high breaches of privilege. A case from Maharashtra, when some M.L.As. were molested and insulted at Nagpur Railway Station in the reservation compartment and later the concerned passengers/officers were punished by the Privileges Committee, is an example.

The Press and Privileges

The Press is often called an extension of Parliament. It is called the 'Fourth Estate' in the United Kingdom. It keeps the people informed of the happenings in Parliament.

However speakers have ruled, that questions, motions and other notices which are merely based on Press reports may not be admitted.

Freedom of speech and expression includes freedom of the Press, and in a Parliamentary system, "The press should enjoy complete freedom to report the proceedings of Parliament fairly and faithfully.... Nobody would deny the Press the right of fair comment. But if the comments contain personal attacks on individual members of Parliament on account of their conduct in Parliament or if the language of the comments is vulgar or abusive, they cannot be deemed to come within the bounds of fair comments or Justifiable criticism."

It is a breach of privilege and contempt of the House to publish expunged proceedings of the House. The Press Reporters in the House meet the concerned officer of the House at about 6.00 p.m. and get authentic information of the expunged proceedings from the day's record. Even some actions, gestures may be expunged.

Freedom from Arrest

The privilege of freedom from arrest is applicable only to civil cases for the duration of the session and for a period of forty days before and forty days after the session. This is to ensure regular attendance of Members in Parliament. This privilege of freedom from arrest does not, however, extend to criminal offences or cases of detention under Preventive Detention.

In case of criminal charge under any law for preventive detention, the House must receive immediate information of the arrest, detention, conviction, imprisonment and release of a member. The failure to do so would constitute a breach of privilege of the House. A member under custody enjoys his right to correspond without any let or hindrance with the Speaker, Secretary or Chairman of a Parliamentary Committee.

A member or a stranger cannot be arrested within the precincts of the House without obtaining the prior permission of the Speaker. There is no specific exemptions from use of handcuffs for Members, but the instructions of sparing the use of handcuffs by the Government are to be followed.

Points of Propriety

There are certain parliamentary practices, usages and conventions which should be followed by the members and others. The violation of such parliamentary practices, usages and conventions does not technically constitute a breach of privilege or contempt of the house but such violation would be termed as impropriety. For example,

Speakers have always ruled that when the House is in session, courtesy and propriety demand that all important announcements regarding policy matters should invariably be made by the Ministers first in the House.

If a Government Officer is unable to accede to the request for help or suggestion of a member, he should explain politely and with courtesy the reasons of his inability to accede to the member's request.

When a member of Parliament or of a State Legislature comes to see a Government Officer, the concerned officer should rise in his seat to receive the member and to see him off. These small gestures have symbolic value and, therefore, the officers are supposed to be meticulously correct and courteous in their dealings with Members of Parliament.

The seating arrangements for members of Parliament at public functions have been clearly brought out in the Table of Precedence approved by the President, which must be followed.

The Government officers should acknowledge promptly letters received from members of Parliament. All such letters should receive careful consideration and should be responded to at an appropriate level expeditiously. To furnish such information or statistics relating to the matters of local importance which may be readily available with them and are not confidential, is also expected.

Some Parliamentary Customs, Conventions and Etiquettes

Like Great Britain, quite a few conventions and etiquettes have developed in our Parliamentary practice. A few related to the Speaker and the House are stated below.

Upon his election, the Speaker is taken to his Chair by the Prime Minister and the Leader of the Opposition. Initially, a Wig and Gown was used by the Speaker, but the first Speaker Shri Mavlankar discarded the tradition as it was unsuitable to our climate. There is no *Mace* on Speaker's Table like that in Great Britain—because we don't have the Committee of the Whole House. The Speaker, while taking his Chair, bows to all sides—first left and then to the right. Shri Sanjeeva Reddy, when he was Speaker, started bowing with folded hands. All Members must bow to the Chair—both while entering and taking seat and while leaving the House, which symbolises respect and permission to the Chair. Pandit Nehru meticulously observed this etiquette. Once, when a Japanese delegation arrived at the airport (behind schedule) and he was informed, he collected papers hastily and started towards the door of the House, but as soon as he remembered, he returned to his seat, bowed to the chair and then left.

No member can get to the Speaker and talk to him. None should distract his attention as he has to be extremely attentive. Members should not turn their backs to the Chair or should not talk away themselves.

Carrying badges of parties etc. or any other article without the permission is not allowed. In the Ninth Lok Sabha an elected Member was not permitted to enter the House with his sword and he declined to be sworn-in as a Member unless permitted to carry it. Ultimately he was not sworn-in. No official dress is allowed but it should be dignified (e.g. not like keeping a coat hanging on shoulders etc.).

Smoking, chewing etc. is not allowed. Sleeping in the House may be connived at but without snoring.

Members should not criticize the rulings given by the Chair. The Member may talk with the Speaker in his Chamber; but this should not be given to press. No allegations can be made against a non-member or a member who is absent in the House.

Unlike Great Britain, our Minister can participate in discussions in other House though they cannot vote there.

There is a Marshal in Lok Sabha who stands near the Speaker's chair, but he is not comparable (as for functions) to the 'Sergeant-at Arms' in the British House of Commons.

The Zero Hour

This is a typical concept which has grown by chance in Indian Parliamentary practice. There is no such provision either in our Constitution or in the Rules etc. of the House. In fact this term was first coined by the Press, but is now in vogue in Parliament and has become a part of the Parliamentary vocabulary. Immediately after the Question Hour i.e. at 12.00 noon, the Members may raise matters of public interest. Any matter which the Member(s) consider important may be taken-up. The Zero hour is non-formalised.

The Cost

The cost for running Parliament's session was calculated (for 1985) at Rs. 965.81 lakhs per session i.e. 3.39 lakhs per day, Rs. 80,000 per hour and Rs. 800 per minute which is minor as compared to other Departments/Ministries etc.

Action on Members for Absence

If a Member remains absent without prior intimation for 60 days, his seat can be declared vacant. A Committee of the House keeps a watch. After continuous absence of 40 days of non-signature a notice is given and after 50 days a telegram reminding the Member of his absence is sent. After 60 days again a telegram is sent. Even then if he does not respond, action follows. In 1985 Subramanian Swami was absent and action was taken under this procedure.

Parliamentary Language

The Members must use parliamentary language and any unparliamentary expressions/terms/phrases/sentences are expunged by the Speaker (in House of Commons expunction is done by the House and not by Speaker) or Member is asked to withdraw his words. Use of terms such as lie, nonsense, foolish etc. is not allowed. While the word 'nonsense' is unparliamentary, the word 'nonsensical' is parliamentary. It also depends upon the context, the style of putting etc. saying 'false' is unparliamentary while 'travelling away from truth' is Parliamentary. At times there is extensive expunction and paragraphs or pages are expunged. There is no specific time-limit for expunctions. Seditious statements or those harming the feelings of communities are expunged. Army is always kept out of discussions. The Speaker's Panel Members function in a very objective manner and Speaker's decision is final. Shri.H.V.R. Aiyangar had said, "Our Speaker has got more powers than those of the Speaker of the House of Commons."

An instance from the British House of Commons is interesting. A Member said, "Half the Members of the House of Commons are fools". This was objected to, but when he said, "Half the Members of the House of Commons are not fools", this was considered parliamentary. We cannot certainly predict as to what view can be taken on such issues.

A Minister who is not a Member and is to get nimself elected within six months also enjoys all Privileges and is also bound by all the limitations of the House.

Citizens can send their petitions to the House through any M.P. who can present it to the Petitions Committee if it is related to any matter of public importance.

No Day

Important issues such as flood, drought etc. may engage the attention of House with Members' consensus and no other work is done.

6

THE PARLIAMENT SECRETARIATS

Presiding Officers' Conference, held in January 1926, adopted a resolution proposing the creation of a separate office for the Central Legislative Assembly, independent of and unconnected with the government. Later on 22 September 1928, Pt. Motilal Nehru moved a resolution in the Central Legislative Assembly to the effect that a separate Assembly Department be constituted. The resolution was adopted unanimously. The Secretary of State for India, accorded his approval (with certain modifications) to the scheme as embodied in the resolution and a separate self-contained department known as the 'Legislative Assembly Department' was created on 10 January 1929, in the portfolio of the Government or General with the Speaker of the Legislative Assembly as its *de facto* head.

The conditions of service of the employees of the Legislative Assembly Department including their recruitment were to be governed by separate Rules called 'The Legislative Assembly Department (Conditions of Service) Rules, 1929. Officers and staff of the Legislative Assembly Department thereafter began to be appointed in accordance with those Rules with the approval of the President (Speaker) of the Assembly. The position and authority of the Speaker in the matter of recruitment, terms and conditions of service of the officers and staff of the Central Assembly Department (and its successor Secretariat) have since been recognised by statutory Rules and Conventions and finally by the Constitution of India.

Under the provisions of the Indian Independence Act, 1947, the Legislative functions of the Central Legislature were taken over by the Constituent Assembly of India. There was, however, no change in the nomenclature of the Legislative Assembly Department. With the coming into force of the Constitution and the creation of a Provisional Parliament on 26 January 1950, the name of the Department was changed to 'Parliament Secretariat'.

Even after the Council of States (Rajya Sabha) and the House of the People (Lok Sabha) came into existence in 1952, the Secretariat of the House of the People continued to be called the 'Parliament Secretariat', and a new Secretariat called the "Council of States Secretariat" was set up for the Rajya Sabha. The names of the two Secretariats were changed in 1954 to Rajya Sabha Secretariat and Lok Sabha Secretariat, respectively.

Separate Secretariats for the two Houses of Parliament were established to ensure that these Secretariats are independent of and unconnected with the government. In fact, the Constitution itself has recognized this paramount need. Article 98 of the Constitution provides that—

> "1. Each House of Parliament shall have a separate staff:
> Provided that nothing in this clause shall be construed as preventing the creation of posts common to both Houses of Parliament.
> 2. Parliament may by law regulate the recruitment, and the conditions of service of persons appointed, to the Secretarial staff of either House of Parliament.
> 3. Until provision is made by Parliament under Clause (2), the President may, after consultation with the Speaker of the House of the People or the Chairman of the Council of States, as the case may be make rules regulating the recruitment, and conditions of service of persons appointed to the Secretarial staff of the House of the People or the Council of States, and any rules so made shall have effect subject to the provisions of any law under the said clause."

The Lok Sabha Secretariat (Recruitment and Conditions of Service) Rules, 1955, were framed Under Article 98(3) and promulgated by the President in consultation with the Speaker. Similarly the Rajya Sabha Secretariat (Recruitment and Conditions of Service) Rules were framed and promulgated in 1957 by the President in consultation with the Chairman.

Though the Constitution of India came into force on 26 January 1950 no law under Article 98(2) has been passed by Parliament so far to regulate the recruitment and conditions of service of persons appointed to the Secretarial staff of Houses of Parliament. Under these circumstances, do the recruitment rules have force of law or not? Dealing with this question, the Committee of Parliament appointed to report on the pay structure of the officers and staff of the Rajya Sabha and Lok Sabha Secretariats and other connected matters had, in para 1.8 of their Report (November 1974), observed that—

> "The Recruitment and Conditions of Service Rules of the Secretariats framed under Constitutional provisions as they are, themselves have the force of law. In any case parliamentary legislation in its very nature would be general and would again need framing of rules thereunder for matters of detail. If on the other hand, details of service conditions etc. were incorporated in the law itself, it would result in a rigid position and amendments involving day-to-day administration of the Secretariats would take a long time to go through the Parliamentary processes, resulting in inordinate delays. The Committee understood that, by experience, the existing Rules had been found to be flexible enough and adequate to meet the requirements of the situation from time to time."

Article 309 of the Constitution makes a provision somewhat similar to Article 98(2) and (3) in respect of the recruitment and conditions of service of persons serving the Union or State Government.

Acts of the appropriate legislature may regulate the recruitment and conditions of service of persons appointed to public services and posts in connection with the affairs of the Union or of any State. It shall be competent for the President or such persons as he may direct in the case of services and posts in connection with the affairs of the Union, and for the Governor of a State or such person as he may direct in the case of services and posts in connection with affairs of the state, to make rules regulating the recruitment and the conditions of service of persons appointed to such services and posts until provision in that behalf is made by or under an Act of the appropriate Legislature under this Article, and any rules so made shall have effect subject to the provisions of any such Act.

It would be seen that no legislation has been passed under this Article, and the recruitment and conditions of service of Government employees continue to be regulated through rules.

It is to ensure the independence of the Secretariats and their officers and staff from the executive Government that the recruitment and conditions of service of their officers and staff are governed by separate Rules made by the President 'after consultation with the Chairman/Speaker' under Article 98(3) of the Constitution. As it is, the Executive has no direct control over the conditions of service of the employees of the Secretariats. The Secretariats function under the ultimate guidance and control of the Chairman/Speaker. Under the Recruitment and Conditions of Service Rules, powers relating to creation of certain permanent and temporary posts, their conversion into permanent ones, the appointment to various posts, the conduct, discipline and control of officers and the regulation of quasi-permanent and temporary services, are vested in the Chairman/Speaker, subject to consultation with the Ministry of Finance as and where specified. Such powers are exercised by the Chairman/Speaker through the issue of Recruitment and Conditions of Service Orders under the Rules.

According to the well-established convention, the orders issued by the Government to the Ministries and Departments of the Government of India do not automatically apply to the officers and staff of the Secretariats. After the promulgation of their recruitment and conditions of service Rules, this position has been formally accepted by the Government Orders issued by the Government in regard to conditions of service of their staff are examined and it is decided to extend the provisions thereof to the officers and staff of the Secretariats, the adaptation orders are issued in the form of Recruitment and Conditions of Service Orders, without again formally consulting the Government. If a financial order is considered necessary, the adaptation order is issued after consultation with the Ministry of Finance.

All matters regulating service conditions form the subject matter of discussion with the Ministry of Finance and if a final settlement at Secretary General's level is not reached, the matter is placed before the Chairman/Speaker, who records his opinion. As a rule, when the Chairman/Speaker is satisfied that certain conditions of service are necessary his opinion prevails. It is, of course, always open to the Minister of Finance to request the Chairman/Speaker to reconsider his decision. In actual practice, such cases have been very rare and the experience of operation of the rules during the last many years has shown that generally no major points of difference arose between the Secretariats and the Ministry of Finance.

It is in keeping in view the independent nature of the Secretariats that the question of revision of pay scales of officers and staff is always kept out side the purview of the Pay Commissions appointed by the Government. Therefore, on the basis of the recommendations made by the pay Commissions in 1946 and in 1957-59, the pay scales of officers and staff of the Secretariats were suitably revised under order issued by the Chairman/Speaker after consulting the Ministry of Finance.

The Third Pay Commission also stated in their report that the employees of the Secretariats of Parliament were excluded from their purview "in view of the provisions of Article 98 of the Constitution". On 16 August 1973, the Speaker, Lok Sabha made an announcement in the House about the appointment of a Committee of Parliament under the Chairmanship of Shri K.N. Tiwari, then Chairman of Estimates Committee. The terms of reference of this Committee were:

> "to advise the Chairman of Rajya Sabha and the Speaker of Lok Sabha on the changes that are considered desirable in the structure of pay and allowances, leave and pensionary benefits to the officers and all categories of staff to the Rajya Sabha and Lok Sabha Secretariats in the context of the decisions of the Government on the recommendations of the Third Pay Commission."

The revised scales of pay as recommended by the Committee of Parliament were introduced w.e.f. 1 December, 1974. It is hoped that similar view will be taken on the recommendation of the Fifth Pay Commission which submitted its report in 1996.

The posts in the Secretariats of the Lok Sabha and the Rajya Sabha have been exempt from the purview of the U.P.S.C. by the U.P.S.C. (Exemption from Consultation) Rules, 1958 promulgated under a notification of the Ministry of Home Affairs. It has also been provided that in the case of orders and other instrument relating to the Secretariats of the Lok Sabha (House of the People) and of the Rajya Sabha (Council of States) the orders in the name of the President could be authenticated by the Officers of the two Secretariats under the Authentications of Orders and Other Instruments Rules, 1958.

In spite of the Constitutional provision, the same situation does not prevail in the State Legislatures.

Organisation of the Secretariat

In December 1974, in pursuance of the recommendation of the Parliamentary Pay Committee, the Lok Sabha Secretariat and the Rajya Sabha Secretariat were reorganised into Services to provide smooth, efficient and effective service to Parliament. In the Lok Sabha Secretariat, the following 11 Services were set up:

(1) *The Legislative Service*
Dealing with the work connected with the business of the House and including Parliamentary Notice Office, Legislative Branch, Table Office, Questions Branch and the Branches dealing with

Legislative Committees, Committee on the Welfare of Scheduled Castes and Scheduled Tribes and Conferences.

(2) *The Financial Committees Service*
Servicing the three Financial Committees viz. Public Accounts Committee, Estimates Committee and Public Undertakings Committee and including the Railway Convention Committee.

(3) *The Executive and Administrative Service*
Including Administration, Works and General, Budget and Payment, Pay and Accounts, Members' Salaries and Allowances, Members' Services and Staff Car Drivers.

(4) *The Library, Research and Information Service*
Consisting of (A) Research and Information Wing and the Press and Public Relations Wing; and (B) Parliament Library Wing (including the Press Clipping, Documentation and Spot Reference Units).

(5) Verbatim Reporting, Personal Secretaries and Stenographic Service.

(6) *Interpretation Service.*

(7) *Printing, Publications, Stationery, Sales, Stores, Distribution and Archives Service.*
Covering (a) Printing, Rota-Printing and Bindery Works, (b) Stationery and Stores, Record-Keeping and Archives, (c) Sales, and (d) Receipt and Distribution.

(8) *Editorial and Translation Service*
Translation of debates, reports and parliamentary papers, editing of debates and writing the synopsis of debates.

(9) *Watch and Ward, Door-Keeper, and Sanitation Service.*

(10) *Clerks, typists record Sorters and Daftries Service.*

(11) *Messengers Service.*

The Bureau of Parliamentary Studies and Training (BPST)

The Bureau of Parliamentary Studies and Training was not amalgamated into any service so that it could grow into and function as an independent wing. It serves the training needs of both the Secretariats.

On the basis of experience gained in the functioning of various services, the three services, namely, the Legislative Service, the Financial Committees Service and Administrative and Executive Service were later merged into one Service.

The Rajya Sabha Secretariat was also reorganized more or less on the same basis. It does not have Financial Committees Service nor

LARRDIS* because the Secretarial assistance to Financial Committees is provided by the Lok Sabha Secretariat and facilities provided by LARRDIS are available to both the Secretariats.

Prior to 1974 the designation of the employees of the two Secretariats were based on status, i.e. Lower Division Clerk, Upper Division Clerk, Assistant, Committee Assistant, Section Officer, Under Secretary, Deputy Secretary, etc. Consequent on reroganisation of the two Secretariats into various services all the posts were redesignated on functional basis. For example, a Deputy Secretary working in the Legislative Service was designated as Chief Examiner of Questions, Chief Examiner of Bills and Motions, Chief Legislative Committee Officer, etc. Deputy Secretaries in the Financial Committees Service were designated as Chief Financial Committee Officer and in the Administrative and Executive Service as Chief Personnel and Executive Officer.

Procedural Reforms

The Lok Sabha Secretariat has been alive to the need for procedural reforms to bring about efficiency and promptitude in disposal of work. Some of the salient reforms introduced and the advantages gained therefrom deserve mention. These are—

(i) The system of putting up self-contained Notes. Such notes have made for disciplined thinking, neat presentation and quick disposal. Such a Note gives at a glance the pros and cons of a problem, the rules on the subject, details of precedents, if any, possible courses of action open. It enables the officers to give a quick decision without raising any queries.

(ii) The 'Jumping Level' system has done away with too many levels of supervision. Now only one person dose the work at the base level, another checks or overseas it, if necessary, and the officer at the third level gives a decision. There is delegation of power, but not a diffusion of responsibility.

(iii) The Diary system under which all communications received in the Secretariat were diarised first in the Distribution Branch and thereafter in the respective Branches, has been abolished. Strange though it may seem, but it is a fact that after abolition of the Diary system, no important latter or note has ever been lost or misplaced.

---

* Library and Reference, Research, Documentation and Information Service.

(iv) In certain areas like Financial Committees and LARRDIS a 'Desk Officer System' has been introduced under which officers themselves do the original work with stenographic assistance.

(v) If a certain thing is not done in time, it is just as well that it is not done at all. The system of marking the files 'Action this Day' has not only been introduced but perfected to such an extent that files carrying such a marking reach the Secretary-General from the lowest officer and whatever may be the levels they have to pass through, these files not only come back the same day to the table of the original officer but action on them is taken the same day.

(vi) Important decisions or documents are extracted from files by Branches and included in the 'Select Documents' or 'Precedent Register' or ' Register of Important Decisions'. This dispenses with the need for recall of old files from the Archives every now and then.

(vii) In 1985, Branches have updated and brought out their 'Practice and Procedure' Volumes. These volumes explain in detail the procedure to be followed by staff in handling various matters dealt with in the Branch.

(viii) Financial Committee Branches and other Committee Branches have brought out 'Introductory Guide' for the benefit of newly elected Members of Eighth Lok Sabha.

(ix) Organisation and Methods (O.&.M) Section of the Secretariat, which was earlier part of the Administrative Service, has been given the functional autonomy it deserves and strengthened to enable it to carry out various studies like Job analysis, fixation of norms, time and motion studies, system of opening and recording of files, etc. and make independent and objective assessment of staff strength.

Nature and Extent of Services and Amenities Provided to Members

Services

The nature and extent of services provided by the officeres and staff to Members are enumerated below :

(i) The proceedings of Lok Sabha are covered verbatim by Parliamentary Reporters. One copy either of the Hindi version or of the English version of Debates and one copy of Index to Debates is supplied free to each Member.

(ii) With a view to save time of the House, an Automatic Vote Recording Equipment has been provided in the Lok Sabha Chamber. This equipment can be used for—
(a) Division; (b) Secret Voting; (c) Quorum.

(iii) The entire proceedings of the House are interpreted simultaneously from Hindi into English and *Vice-Versa* by Parliamentary Interpreters and can be followed by Members in English or Hindi by using headphones and by operating the language selector switch installed at every seat in the Chamber. Arrangements also exist for providing simultaneous interpretation into English and Hindi of speeches made in a few regional languages.

(iv) Parliamentary Notice Office in Parliament House receives all Notices and communications from Members, supplies forms therefor, issues Identity Cards-cum-Railway Passes, Spouse Railway passes, CGHS cards and visitors cards, attends to various queries by Members and renders general assistance to Members in regard to Parliamentary work.

(v) The following Parliamentary papers are circulated to Members at their residences:

(a) List of Business,
(b) List of Questions,
(c) Bulletin Part I & II,
(d) Bills introduced in Rajya Sabha,
(e) Bills to the introduced in the House,
(f) Bills passed by Rajya Sabha and laid on the Table of the House which are to be considered by the House,
(g) Lists of amendments to Bills, Resolutions & Motions,
(h) Lists of Cut Motions, and
(i) Reports of Certain Parliamentary Committees.

(vi) The Parliamentary Library and Reference, Research, Documentation and Information Service serves Members of Parliament by providing *inter alia* research and reference materials on legislative measures and other important matters coming up for discussion before the two Houses of Parliament. The Service is divided into four Divisions:

(a) Library Division,
(b) Reference and Documentation Division,
(c) Research and Information Division (A), and

(d) Research and Information Division (B).

(vii) A 'Synopsis' giving the gist of important suggestions and points made during the debate (other than Question and Answers) is prepared, printed and supplied to Members daily. It is brought out in English and Hindi.

(viii) The Bureau of Parliamentary Studies and Training holds seminars for Members of Parliament and State Legislatures on various subjects of Parliamentary interest and conducts orientation programmes for newly elected Members of Parliament.

(ix) The Indian Parliamentary Group, an autonomous body formed in 1949, in pursuance of a motion adopted by the Constituent Assembly (on 16 August 1948, promotes personal contacts between members of Parliament and arranges seminars and discussions on subject of Parliamentary interest. It also arranges visits to foreign countries. The Group functions as the National Group of the Inter-Parliamentary Union and as main branch of the Commonwealth Parliamentary Association in India.

(x) The officers and staff of the Watch and Ward, Door-Keeper and Sanitation Service ensure security of Members, guard the precincts of Parliament House and maintain highest standard of sanitation.

(xi) The Editorial and Translation Service provides translation of all parliamentary papers e.g. List of Business, Bulletins, Question lists, Debates, Notices, Minutes of sittings and Reports of Parliamentary Committees etc.

The Members of Parliament are paid salary, allowances and pension under the provisions of the Salary, Allowances and Pensions of Members of Parliament to Act, 1954, as amended, and the rules made thereunder. Every Member is issued Identity Card-cum-Railway Pass, Spouse Railway Pass, Steamer Pass, Spouse Steamer Pass. Members can obtain Air Tickets from the Indian Airlines on credit basis on production of Exchange orders issued by the Secretariat. Other amenities to Members include allotment of accommodation, telephones at their usual place of residence and in Delhi, Medical facilities, railway and air reservations, Banking and postal facilities, bus transport facilities, catering facilities, Super Bazar facilities etc.

SECRETARY GENERAL OF THE LOK SABHA

The Secretary-General of Lok Sabha must possess certain special abilities, characteristics and aptitude. It is an office with great responsibility. The role of Secertary-General in the Parliamentary set-up is a vital one though there is no statutory provision. He continues from Parliament to Parliament. He may be called a repository of the accumulated wisdom of the House, the custodian of its culture and traditions and a link between succeeding House and their changing membership. He heads the Secretariat which serves the supreme representatives of the people, without any partiality to their political views or their party affiliations. The evolution of the office over the years has witnessed accretion to its duties, functions and responsibilities.

The Government of India Act, 1919 which gave effect to the Montague-Chelmsford Reforms, established for the first time a bicameral legislature at the Center comprising of the Legislative Assembly and the Council of States. The Secretary to the Government of India in the legislative department was Secretary of both the Houses and was appointed by order by the Governor-General and held office during his pleasure. In this scheme of things, the Secretary of the Assembly owed no allegiance to the Assembly or to the President of the Assembly. He was, for all practical purposes, responsible to the Governor-General in Council. He was a nominated member of the House, and as such, was a member of a party, voted with his party and worked for his party. In this position, the President (Speaker) could not regard the advice of the Secretary in connection with the business of the House as coming from a wholly impartial, unbiased and independent source.

The Legislative Assembly was conscious of the need for an independent status for its Secretariat since its inception in 1921. From time to time, the subject matter was raised in the Assembly through questions and resolutions. A beginning in the direction of the autonomy was first made when September 1928, the Viceroy discontinued the practice of nominating the Secretary as a member of the Assembly. On 10 January 1929, a self-contained department known as the 'Legislative Assembly Department' was created in the portfolio of the Governor-General with the President (Speaker) of the Legislative Assembly as its *de-facto* head. In accordance with the Legislative Assembly Department (Condition of Service Rules), 1929 framed by the Secretary of State in Council, the Officers of the House were appointed by the Governor-General after consulation with the President and the President was, under the above Rules, entitled to sit with the

Federal Public Service Commission at the interviews for the selection of personnel for his Department. After independence, the independant position of the Secretariat was constitutionally safeguarded under Clause (1) of Article 98 of the Constitution, which came into force on 26 January, 1950. The recruitment and conditions of service of persons appointed to the Secretariat are now regulated in accordance with the Lok Sabha Secretariat (Recruitment and Conditions of Service) Rules, 1955 which were issued by the President, after consultation with the Speaker of Lok Sabha under Clause (3) of Article 98. The Secretary-General who, till October 1973, was designated Secretary, heads the Secretariat of the Lok Sabha (House of the People) under the overall direction of the Speaker.

The Secretary-General is a permanent officer of the House and is selected and appointed by the Speaker from amongst those who have made their mark in the service of Parliament in various capacities. Once appointed, he remains in his post until he attains the prescribed age of retirement.

The Position of the Secretary-General

His position is unique, as he is a leading public servant, firstly, because it is his function to ensure the administration and working of Lok Sabha which is a supreme body, representative of the people, constituted by direct elections on the basis of adult suffrage. He has to see that the correct observance of Parliamentary procedure is ensured.

He also enjoys his position by virtue of his political impartiality. In the Warrant of Precedence, he holds the same rank as prescribed for Secretaries to the Government of India. He is answerable only to the Speaker and his action cannot be discussed either inside or outside the House. In his capacity as the Secretary-General of the House, he is an officer of the House and enjoys the privilege of freedom from arrest except on a criminal charge. He cannot be obstructed in the execution of his duty, as it would amount to contempt of the House. The House treats as breach of its privilege not only acts directly tending to obstruct the Secretary-General or other Officers in the performance of their duty but also any conduct which may tend to deter them from doing their duty.

Functions of Secretary-General

The functions of the Secretary-General may be broadly classified into two categories.

(1) Parliamentary,
(2) Administrative.

(1) Parliamentary Functions

His functions in this sphere are very important. He is expected to know everything that has any reference to Lok Sabha and its business, be it an abstruse constitutional point or the proper precedents that should be followed in any given circumstances. In resolving doubts and interpreting the Rules, the Secretary-General with his vast experience and knowledge of precedents and conventions, is able to suggest to the Speaker the most appropriate solution. Anticipating the happenings during the day and with a capacity to apply Rules to the ever-changing phenomena, he tenders advice to smoothen any complex situation that might arise in the House. He is all the time conscious that his advice has to be reasonable and accurate. His various functions in the sphere of Parliament may be broadly classified us under:

(i) Relations with the Speaker

The Secretary-General is the adviser to the Speaker in the matter of exercise of all the powers and functions that belong to the Speaker, and to the House through the Speaker. He acts under the authority and in the name of the Speaker but does not work under delegated authority. The orders passed by the Secretary-General are the orders in the name of the Speaker and the Speaker accepts full responsibility for those orders. No two persons are more closely associated in their work than the Speaker and the Secretary-General. A relationship of utmost confidence in each other has to exist. It is a delicate and personal relationship which is not susceptible to any accurate description.

What emerges out of this close relationship is the area of demarcation in the disposal of work concerning parliamentary and administrative matters. Normally the Secretary-General, subject to any specific directions of the Speaker, determines what matters he will place before the Speaker and what matters he would dispose of himself. In cases of doubt and difficulty, however, he consults the Speaker.

(ii) Morning Meeting with Speaker

The meeting of Secretary-General with the Speaker daily an hour before the commencement of sitting of the House is the most crucial hour of a day in Parliamentary work. A spate of notices of adjournment motions, calling attention and other matters of urgent public importance pour in at that time requiring immediate attention; there is no time to deal with them at length. They are discussed verbally by the Secretary-General with the Speaker in the latter's Chamber, supported by previous rulings, precedents and conventions wherever possible and quick decisions are taken as to the manner of their disposal. The pith and substance of the decision on each matter is crystallised just in a few words which help the Speaker to give his decisions in the Chamber or rulings in the House.

(iii) In the House

The Secretary-General is present in the House during the sittings of Lok Sabha. He occupies a seat just below the desk of the Speaker in the pit of the Chamber and is even otherwise constantly available to the Speaker for consultation. In the course of the debate, the Speaker, on many occasions, has to take decisions on the spot and give rulings in cases involving interpretation of the Rules. Although he is guided by precedents, their application creates ticklish problems as they are to be applied in the background and the circumstances peculiar to each case.

Quite often one witnesses an exciting or a pulsating moment in the House with which the speaker comes to grip and with which the Secretary-General keeps in tune. In such a fluid state, when new facts emerge in quick succession one has to gauge the collective mind of the House, recall the precedents and apply the Rules so as to arrive at an almost instant decision. In deciding the matter in that fleeting moment, one should not be swayed away by the emotional feelings of the House and the Procedural aspect must always have precedence. This is all the more essential, as certainty of procedure is very vital to the functioning of Parliament. Advice tendered by the Secretary-General in that behalf is of considerable importance. In such delicate situations one witnesses the Secretary-General occasionally passing on information and advice to the Speaker through the Marshal, through slips of paper or by personally going over to the Speaker to whisper some points to help him to give immediate rulings. The Secretary-General does not impose his suggestions. Being the principal adviser to the Presiding Officer, he merely offers his opinion and it is for the latter to accept it or not.

(iv) With the Members

The Secretary-General's advice is available to all members, irrespective of party affiliation. The task is difficult and delicate in nature, as he has not only to hold a balance between the Government and the opposition but must also enjoy the confidence of both. He never gives advice unless asked for. When asked, the advice is full and frank and completely impartial. Sitting in the House, he is not parimarily concerned with politics but functions in the midst of an institution which is intimately connected with politics.

The Secretary-General has to be alert all the time, watch the situation, understand the members' viewpoints, enjoy the confidence of the Speaker and give advice which is not only procedurally correct but also politically feasible so as to meet thee challenges of the developing political situation. What is vital at this juncture is an attitude of objectivity, a sense of fairness coupled with ready wit at his command to smoothen the situation. Indeed the application of these qualities is an art which he acquires by practice and experience. In sum, the office of the Secretary-General is one of offices in which development of one's own character and personality is of crucial importance.

(v) Other Parliamentary Functions

Some of the Parliamentary duties of the Secretary-General are laid down in the Rules of Procedure and Conduct of Business in Lok Sabha, but many others are performed by practice and convention. When President arrives to address both Houses of Parliament assembled together, the Secretaries-General of the two Houses along with the Chairman, Rajya Sabha and Speaker, Lok Sabha receive the President at the gate of Parliament House and come to the Central Hall in a procession along with the President. Similarly, they join the procession when the President departs. For the purpose of elections to the offices of the President and the Vice-President, the Secretaries-General of Lok Sabha and Rajya Sabha are alternately appointed as Returning Officers.

Whenever a session of the House is to be held, the Secretary-General issues, on the basis of orders passed by the President, summons to each member attend the session. When new Lok Sabha meets after a general election, the Secretary-General lays on the Table a list of members elected to Lok Sabha which is presented to the Speaker by the Chief Election Commissioner. After the conclusion of the

President's Address to both Houses of Parliament after a general election or at the first session of each year, the Secretary-General lays on the Table a copy each of Hindi and English version of the Address duly authenticated by the President.

He keeps a roll of members of the House which must be signed, in his presence, by every newly elected member before taking his seat. He also causes to send to every member notice of the date for the election of the Speaker and the Deputy Speaker, and receive notices which any member may give proposing names for these offices.

He is responsible for the arrangement of government business in such order as the Speaker may, after consultation with the Leader of the House, determine and for the preparation of a list of business for each day of the session. He circulates the list of business, lists of admitted questions as also every bulletin, list of amendments notice or other paper which is required to be made available to members under the Rules. The Rules also provide that every notice like notice of question, motion, resolution, Bill, Amendment, question of privilege, adjournment motion, matters of urgent public importance for short duration discussion etc. has to be given by members in writing addressed to the Secretary-General.

Where the previous sanction or recommendation of the President is required under the Constitution for the introduction or consideration of a Bill or moving of an amendment thereto or the consideration of a Demand for Grant, the Minister or member concerned has to communicate in writing to the Secretary-General the President's sanction or recommendation.

The Secretary-General signs messages communicated from the Lok Sabha to Rajya Sabha if it is in session, otherwise forwards them to each member through the Bulletin and certifies all Bills to be transmitted or returned to Rajya Sabha. In case of urgency, he authenticates Bills in the absence of the Speaker before these are presented to the President for assent and lays them on the Table of the House after they are assented to by him.

In case of joint sittings of the two Houses, the Presiding Officer is the Speaker and the responsibility for organising the concerned Secretarial work devolves upon the Secretary-General. In that connection, he issues summons to the members of both the Houses and causes to be prepared a full report of the proceedings of every sitting and have it published in such form and manner as the Speaker may direct.

The Secretary-General receives petitions, documents and papers addressed to or intended for the House and reports to the House any such petitions etc. received by him and admitted by the Speaker. He issues passes for the admission of visitors to the galleries. He has the custody of all records, documents and papers of the House or any of its Committees or the Secretariat and does not permit any such paper to be taken out from the Parliament House without the permission of the Speaker.

A Minister wishing to correct any inaccuracy in the information given by him in answer to a starred or unstarred or short notice or supplementary question or in debate has to give notice to the Secretary-General of his intention to correct it accompanied by a copy of the statement in regard thereto.

In case of a member's resignation of his seat in the House or where a seat is declared vacant by the House, the Secretary-General causes the information to be published in the Gazette and forwards a copy of the notification to the Election Commission for taking steps to fill the vacancy thus caused.

Maintenance of order in the precincts of Parliament House comes under the domain of the Speaker. Secretary-General looks after the Security arrangements in Parliament House and keeps the Speaker posted with all important developments and arrangements. Visitors are admitted to the Galleries on visitors cards issued in the name of the Secretary-General. Similarly, Identity Cards cum Railway passes to Members and their spouses are also issued in the name of Secretary-General.

By virtue of his being Secretary-General of all Parliamentary committees he may attend the meetings of such committees himself or cause his officers to attend them. He is empowered to fix the date and time of a sitting of a Parliamentary committee, if the Chairman of that committee, is not readily available. In case of a Select or Joint Committee on a Bill, he does so in consultation with the Minister-in-charge of the Bill. When it is considered necessary to take evidence of a witness, the Secretary-General issues summons to the witness to appear before the House or Committee thereof. If a Parliamentary Committee completes its report and the Lok Sabha is dissolved in the mean time, the Secretary-General lays that report on the Table of the new House at the first convenient opportunity, and while laying it he makes a statement to the effect that the report was presented to the Speaker of the preceding Lok Sabha. Where it is ordered by the Speaker that the report be previously printed, published or circulated, the Secretary-General also reports that fact to the House.

In the event of quorum not being present at the time appointed for commencement of the sitting of the House even after the quorum bell has been rung thrice, the Secretary-General brings the matter to the notice of the Speaker and under his orders informs the members present in the House about the time when the house will meet next.

(2) Administrative Functions

The Secretary-General heads the Lok Sabha Secretariat which is independent of the Executive and which functions under the overall direction of the Speaker. This ensures that the House is assured of independent advice and its directions are executed without any interference from outside.

As the administrative head of the Secretariat of the House, the Secretary-General exercises the powers vested in the Speaker including the determination of the strength, method of recruitment and of qualifications etc. for the various categories of posts. He is the appointing, punishing and appellate authority for all classes of officers. The rules of conduct, of discipline and control over the officers and staff of the Secretariat are enforced by him. He exercises financial powers and initiates Budget proposals relating to Lok Sabha and its Secretariat. He is the Chief Accounting Authority for the money sanctioned by the House for expenditure under the Demands for Grants of Lok Sabha and its Secretariat, and responsibility is discharged by him through and with the assistance of the Pay and Accounts Officer who works in direct relation with him.

He authenticates the order of the President and the Speaker, corresponds direct with the Ministries and Departments of the Government of India and State and foreign Governments and legislatures on behalf of Lok Sabha and its Secretariat. He also corresponds with members including Ministers in connection with the business of the House or any matter likely to come up before the House.

Other Secretarial functions are in the sphere of Conferences of Presiding Officers of Legislative Bodies of India, and other conferences like the Conferences of Chairmen of Public Accounts Committee, Committee on Subordinate Legislation etc. arranging extra-parliamentary activities such as addersses by distinguished persons, sending of Parliamentary delegations or goodwill missions or receiving such missions from foreign countries to India. He also functions as the *ex-officio* Secretary of the Indian Parliamentary Group (which acts both as the National Group of the Inter-Parliamentary Union and also as the (India Branch of the Commonwealth Parliamentary Association) and its Executive Committee.

In order to keep the members well informed of the day-to-day developments in India and abroad, an up-to-date and well-equipped library is maintained with an efficient Research and Information Service under the overall supervision and guidance of the Secretary-General. The service functions on the lines of the subject-section-cum-desk officer or desk-section system with each of the Sections or Desks being responsible for certain specified subject-areas and Ministries or Departments of the Government of India. The reference wing provides reference material on legislative measures and other matters coming up before the House so as to enable members to participate effectively in the debates. Quite often members are supplied with material at extremely short notice and sometimes actually while the debate is going on in the House.

The Research and Information Division aims at assessing in advance the needs of the Legislators by identifying the topics of current interest on which there is likely to be a more general demand for information and keeps them informed by the timely issue of Bibliographies, Documentation lists, Brochures, Background Notes, Information Bulletins, Fact sheets and Current Information Digests.

While selecting subjects for preparing the above, the effort is to cover as wide a field as possible, keeping in view the members' information needs and the subjects currently agitating the public mind. From time to time, the Division is entrusted with Special assignments of preparing Briefs, Background Papers and Research Notes for the various Parliamentary Conferences and for the goodwill delegations of members of Parliament going abroad. It also assists various Committees of Parliament by making available to them specialized notes and other material as and when required. At each stage the Secretary-General is intimately involved in taking policy decisions, giving appropriate directions, examining and approving manuscripts of research projects etc. and guiding the senior research staff in various ways. Apart from bringing out periodicals like the *Digests of Central Acts and of Legislative and Constitutional Cases and Abstracts of Books, Reports and Articles, Monthly Diary of Political Events and Digest of News and Views on Public Undertakings,* the Secretary-General himself edits the *Quarterly Journal of Parliamentary Information* and the *Hindi Quarterly Sansadiya Patrika.* All these have proved to be of immense value to the members in the discharge of their Parliamentary duties

Bureau of Parliamentary Studies and Training (BPST)

Under the overall control and guidance of the Secretary-General, a

Bureau of Parliamentary Studies and Training has been set up to provide necessary opportunities of training, orientation and study in parliamentary institutions and procedures.

Parliamentary Museum and Archives

India has all along attached utmost importance to parliamentary institutions. Of late, efforts are being made to harness all necessary resources towards salvaging, collecting and preserving for the present and future generations the country's rich heritage in this area. A beginning was made in 1976 when the Lok Sabha Secretariat set up a Parliamentary Archives of Photographs and Films to preserve an authentic, comprehensive, complete and up-to-date pictorial record of the history of the institutions of Parliament, its activities and personalities. A proposal for setting up a Parliamentary Museum and Archives was approved by the General Purposes Committee of the Lok Sabha on 1 August 1984. The basic aim of the Parliamentary Museum and Archives is to preserve the past and the present for the future by protecting from the ravages of time and neglect of all the precious records, historic documents and articles connected with the Constitution and the Parliament and through them to make the history and growth of parliamentary institutions and the political system better understood.

Hall of National Achievements

The General Purpose Committee of the Lok Sabha, on 1 August 1984, approved a proposal for the establishment of a Hall of National Achievements which envisages to present an overall picture of the progress to the nation has achieved in diverse fields ever since independence. It is proposed to present through exhibition, models, photographs and other visual materials a panoramic view of India's achievements since Independence. The underlying idea is to project through audio-visual means an integrated and healthy image of the country to members of foreign parliamentary delegations, visiting dignitaries, students, tourists coming to Delhi and others.

The Parliamentary Museum and Archives and the Hall of National Achievements too function under the overall guidance and control of the Secretary-General.

Secretary General of the Rajya Sabha

The Secretary-General of the Council of States (Rajya-Sabha) also enjoys the same position and performs similar functions as the Secretary-General of Lok Sabha. The post was formally given its present designation viz. Secretary-General with effect from November 1973. He is a permanent officer of the House and is appointed by the Chairman of Rajya Sabha and remains in office till retirement after completing 60 years of age. He is answerable only to the Chairman and has a rank equivalent to other Secretaries in Executive Departments. He Performs Parliamentary functions for the Rajya Sabha and administrative functions for his Secretariat which are on similar lines as those of the Secretary-General of Lok Sabha.

Role of the Secretary-General(s)

R.R. James in his book *An Introduction to the House of Commons* writes:

> "At two O'clock on every sitting day, the clerk and the Speaker hold a Conference in the Speaker's House, when they go through the business for the day and attempt to foresee any difficulties which may arise. In the case of the Report stage of Bill, the Speaker is given a marked copy of the Amendments, explaining the history of each one if it was discussed for five hours in the committee and defeated on a division; if the Minister promised to 'look at it again', or whatever the circumstances may—so that he (Speaker) is adequately seized of the implications of each amendment..... In the House he (Secretary-General) can lean back in his Chair, and whisper to the Speaker or get up and stand beside the Chair: Such hurried discussions do not occur very often, and on at least one occasion, it was not of much assistance. Speaker Dension asked the clerk Sir Denis Le Merchant, when a storm arose in the House. "I recommend you Sir, to be very cautious, "whispered the clerk and disappeared."

Parliamentary activity is vast and varied and contribution of the Secretary-General to raise the highest representative institution of the country in the eyes of the public is not insignificant. Whether while occupying his place at the Table, assisting the Committees or dealing with the day-to-day business of the House, his functions demand great qualities of judgement and maturity of thought. His decisions have to be based on sincerity of purpose and impartiality of outlook, and his work characterised by a great spirit of devotion and attachment to the Parliamentary institutions and sometimes carried out under difficult conditions. In a very full sense, the Secretary-General is the repository of the accumulated wisdom of the House, the custodian of culture and traditions and the one continuing link between the succeeding Houses and their changing membership. That is how he carves out a place for himself in the estimation of the House and leaves his imprint on democratic and Parliamentary institutions and processes.

The Secretary-General plays an important role in raising the prestige of Parliament in the eyes of the public. Whether seated at the Table, assisting the committees or dealing with the day-to-day functioning of the house, the Secretary-General becomes very well known to members who turn to him for advice on points of Parliamentary law and procedure. His decisions always reflect a sincerity of purpose and his outlook bears the stamp of impartiality. In conclusion the following observations of Speaker V.J. Patel which were made as early as 1929, are relevant even today:

> "It is the duty of the Secretary to study every motion and amendment and consider whether ; it is in order or not. The Secretary should also anticipate objection likely to be raised in the House in connection with the business of the day, he should then bring such points as he considers necessary to the notice of the Speaker and discuss them with him, before the House sits. He should be ready whenever possible with the previous rulings and precedents and also parliamentary authorities. He must not forget that the Secretary is the only person who can advise the Speaker in all these matters and therefore, it is his duty to prepare himself to be useful to him. The best and the easiest course is for the Secretary to discuss verbally all questions with the Speaker. It is necessary in the interest of the smooth working of the Department that the Officers of the Department who pass any orders in connection with any business of the Assembly must always bear in mind that the responsibility of such orders is that of the Speaker."

7

THE SUPREME COURT AND THE PARLIAMENT

The Basic requirements of a federal polity are—

(i) a written and a rigid Constitution,
(ii) a scheme of distribution of powers between the Union and the States, and
(iii) a Supreme Court with an independent status.

Though our federal structure deviates from the model of the American federation, so much so that Prof. K.C. Wheare prefers to call it a 'quasi-federal state', we do have a written and a partially rigid Constitution, an elaborate distribution of powers in three exhaustive lists viz. the Union list, the State List and the Concurrent List (with an edge to the Centre over States) and a Supreme Court which heads the independent judiciary common for the Union and the States.

The process of amendment prescribes a procedure which is different from that of the law-making process and some what more difficult than it. Specially for certain Articles it is more difficult as 50 per cent of the State Legislatures must concur in addition to the usual special majority in both Houses of Parliament. This clearly shows that the ordinary law-making process is different from the process prescribed under Article 368 for amending the Constitution. As a result, there is a difference between Laws passed by the Parliament and the Constitutional law or Constitutional Amendment, much unlike Great Britain, where there is no written Constitution and no difference between the law-making power and Constitutional amendment. In India the Law of the Constitution is the basic or fundamental law and is superior to the ordinary laws passed by the Parliament. As a result, the Indian Parliament or any State Legislature is not and cannot be 'sovereign' in the British sense, because any law repugnant to the Constitution will be *ultra vires* and hence void.

The Supreme Court

An independent judiciary headed by a Supreme Court heads the judiciary consisting of High Courts and subordnate courts. Judges are appointed by the President and can be removed only by him on a recommendation made by special majority in both Houses of Parliament. They retire on attaining 65 years of age. They are paid high salaries which are non-votable and charged on the Consolidated Fund of India. By giving high status and dignity the much needed independence is maintained.

The First ever Impeachment of a Judge

The First ever Impeachment of a Supreme Court judge was initiated against Justice Ramaswamy of the Supreme Court after a panel of three judges appointed by the Ninth Lok Sabha submitted its report fixing eleven charges against him. Voting on the motion of impeachment took place on 11th May 1993 in Lok Sabha. The Congress (I) members including the Prime Minister Narasimha Rao and all his Ministers (in all 207 Members) abstained from voting while 198 Members supported the motion. The first ever impeachment motion on a judge thus failed.

Primacy of the Opinion of the Chief Justice of India

A significant judgment was delivered by the Supreme Court of India on 5 October 1993 putting its seal of primacy to the opinion of the Chief Justice of India over the political executive on the key issue of appointment and transfer of judges of Supreme Court and High Courts. The Supreme Court thus revised its earlier decision in the S.P. Gupta case. By a majority of seven-two, the nine-judge Constitution bench of the Supreme Court held that the appointment of judge made to the Supreme Court and High Courts shall be in conformity with the opinion of the Chief Justice of India, arrived at by a process of consultation with other Constitutional functionaries under Articles 124(2) and 217(1) of the Constitution. In the S.P. Gupta case the Court had held that the role of Chief Justice in the consultation process did not assume primacy, either in the appointment or their transfer.

The Judgment says the initiation of the proposal for appointment of the judges to the Supreme Court or for the transfer of the Chief

Justice or a Judge of a High Court must be made by the Chief Justice of India. The only condition imposed on the Chief Justice of the Supreme Court by this judgment is that he should arrive at a conclusion on appointment of judges in consultation with two of his senior most brother Judges.

The judgment said that in the event of conflicting opinion by the Constitutional functionaries, the opinion of the judiciary symbolised by the view of the Chief Justice of India, and formed by consultation with senior judges of the Supreme Court (as stated above) shall have primacy. The Court made it clear that no appointment of any judge to the Supreme Court or the High Courts can be made unless it was in conformity with the opinion of the Chief Justice of India.

Jurisdiction

The Supreme Court of India has original as well as appellate jurisdiction.

Under its original jurisdiction the function is that of a federal tribunal. All disputes between the Union and a State, the Union and one or many states versus one or many states and between one or many states versus one or many states, originate before this Court and its decisions are final.

The Court also has a jurisdiction to entertain petitions for implementation of fundamental rights of citizens (Articles 32) which runs concurrent with that of High Courts (under Article 226).

The Court is the sole arbiter to decide all cases regarding the election to the posts of President and Vice-President of India.

The appellate jurisdiction of this Court covers appeals from High Courts which include those involving Constitutional interpretation or some such basic point (Article 132), civil appeals and criminal appeals, either with or without certificate of the High Courts (in such cases the Supreme Court may certify it on the merits of the case).

The Supreme Court has got a consultative jurisdiction. The President of India may under Article 143 of the Constitution refer a dispute for opinion to the Supreme Court. Though the opinion of the Court is not binding on the President (the Constitution does not provide that it is binding), but it has a pursuasive authority. It is the duty of the Court to tender such advice. Many such cases have been referred to the Supreme Court so far, e.g., the Indo-Pak agreement on transfer of Beru-Bari and Cooch Bihar enclaves (1960); the conflict between the U.P. Legislature and High Court of Allahabad (1964); Special Courts Bill, 1978 (1979) and the Cauvery Water Dispute between

Karnataka and Tamil Nadu States (1991).

The Supreme Court has got the power to review its own judgments (Article 145). Thus, in Golaknath Case the Court overruled the decisions in Shankari Prasad Singh vs. Union of India and Sajjan Singh vs. State of Rajasthan, but in Keshavanand Bharati vs. State of Kerala case, the Supreme Court overruled the decision in the Golaknath case. Hence 'the principle of *stare decisis* is accepted as a principle of policy but not as a mechanical formula' which may collide or confront with better and sounder principles and experience.

From a Jurisdiction point of view, its discretion to grant special leave of appeal against any judgment, order etc. by any Court in India (Article 136) assumes special significance. Its jurisdiction may be enlarged by parliament by law, to include any matter included in the Union List.

Judicial Review

The judgment delivered by C.J. John Marshall of the United States Supreme Court in 1803 in the famous case *Marbury* v. *Madison* ushered in a new era in the role of the Supreme Court. The power of judicial review which empowers the American Supreme Court to review the Laws passed by the Congress and orders of the President in the context of the interpretation which the Court gives to the Constitution and to declare them *ultra vires* of the Constitution and hence void, springs from the doctrine of implied powers. On the contrary, the judicial review available to the Supreme Court in India of the Central as well as State Laws and Executive Orders/Ordinances etc. has its origin in some of the specific provides in our Constitution.

The power of Indian Supreme Court to declare legislative enactments invalid is expressly provided in Article 13 which declares that every law in force or every future law inconsistent with or in derogation of the Fundamental Rights, shall be void, and Article 32 vests in the Supreme Court the power to enforce these rights. Articles 131 and 136 dealing with the jurisdiction of the court expressly vest in the Supreme Court the same power of reviewing legislative enactments of the Union and the States. Article 132 empowers it to interpret the Constitution.

The division of powers under Article 246 between the Union and the States also makes the Supreme Court the sole arbiter. Some hold the view that the power of judicial review in India is as wide in scope as in the United States. Dr. Ambedkar had urged the Court to go into the spirit of the Constitution rather than the words. In 1950,

Justice S.R. Das maintained, "....Chief Justice Marshall assumed the power to declare any law unconstitutional on the ground of its not being in 'due process of law', an expression found in the Fifth Amendment of their Constitution. In India, the expression used is 'the procedure established by law'. Hence when the legislatures are within their legislative limits, the court has no authority to question the wisdom or policy of the law duly made by the appropriate legislature . . . In India the position of Judiciary is somewhere between the Courts in England and the United States . . . Our Constitution, unlike the English Constitution, recognises the Court's Supremacy over the legislative authority, but such supremacy is a very limited one, for, it is confined to the field where the legislative power is circumscribed by limitations put upon it by the Constitution itself." Within this restricted field, the Court may, on a scrutiny of the law made by the Legislature, declare it void if it is found to have transgressed the constitutional limitations.

While the American Constitution is a Brief document, believing in omissions, the Indian Constitution is a document which gives details about structures and provisions thus reducing the scope of interpretation to the Court as compared to the American Supreme Court.

However, some authorities state that the Supreme Court of India has wider powers than the Supreme Court of the United States of America, the Supreme Court of Canada and the High Court of Austrilia.[1] The doctrine of *ultra vires* which is implicit in the working of a federal polity is emphasised in the Indian Constitution as judicial review and is formally embodied in the Constitution.

In Britain, the doctrine of Parliamentary Supremacy still holds good. No court of law there can declare a law of Parliament as invalid. Every Court is constrained to enforce every provision of law of Parliament. Under the Indian Constitution, Parliament is not supreme as, firstly, there is division of powers between the Union and the States, restricting the scope a Parliament's power as per the list(s), and secondly, due to the Fundamental Rights (except in cases of laws passed to implement any of the Directive Principles of State Policy given in Part (IV) which are protected by the Supreme Court against every form a legislative encroachment. Thus, though our Constitution has adopted the Parliamentary system it has not accepted the English doctrine of supremacy of Parliament in matters of legislation. In this respect it has followed the American Constitution (J.B.K. Mukherjea—1950, S.C.J. 262) and hence is more akin to it than the English or any other Constitution. An ordinary law passed by simple majority (like that in Britain) may change a few less significant Articles, or an amendment passed by a special majority in both houses of Parliament can change certain provisions of the Constitution while in case of some Articles this must be consented to by 50 per cent of State Legislatures.

The high-water mark of judicial creativity was reached in some landmark cases like Golaknath case (AIR, 1967, S.C., 1669), Keshavanand Bharati case (AIR,1973, S.C., 1461) and Maneka Gandhi case (AIR, 1978, S.C. 597). In these cases the Supreme Court has emphasized that in India the Constitution is Supreme and that a statute law to be valid must in all cases be in conformity with the constitutional limits and if it transgresses such limits, it is for the Court, which is bound by oath to uphold the Constitution, to declare such law unconstitutional. The First and Seventh Amendments to the Constitution affecting Fundamental rights were challenged in Shankari Prasad vs. Union of India (1952) and Sajjan Singh vs. State of Rajasthan (1965) on the ground that the Parliament had no power to abridge/fundamental Rights, and that the word 'Law' in Article 13(2) includes 'amendment'. In Golaknath Case (1967) the Supreme Court overruled the above two decisions and the majority judgment held that Parliament had on power to take away or abridge the Fundamental rights; and that the word 'Law' in Article 13(2) included amendment of the Constitution and that Article 368 contained only procedure for amendment and did not contain substantive powers of amendment. This decision was overruled by the Supreme Court in the Keshavanand Bharati case which upheld the Twenty-Fourth Amendment and held that in exercise of the power of Amendment, Parliament can amend any article including the Fundamental Rights. Thus the decision in Golaknath case was nullified in so far as the full bench of thirteen judges of the Supreme Court ruled (in Keshavanand Bharati case) unanimously that the Twenty-Fourth Amendment was valid and Articles 368 and 13(2) could be amended. The ambit of power of Article 368 was upheld so far as its scope to all parts of the Constitution was concerned. Seven judges held that the Fundamental Rights can be amended but they being a part of the essential elements or the *basic structure* of the Constitution, cannot be abrogated or destroyed by the exercise of the power of amendment under Article 368. In the words of J. Khanna (one of these seven judges). "The power of amendment under Article 368 did not include the power to abrogate the Constitution. Nor did it include the power to alter the basic structure of framework of the Constitution. Subject to this, power of amendment is plenary." (Six judges held that there were these limitations or restrictions on the amending power under Article 368.)

The Maneka Gandhi case (1978) is a landmark in the post-emergency period. In this case the Court re-interpreted the expression 'the procedure established by law' in Article 21 and held that the Procedure "cannot be arbitrary, unfair or unreasonable". The Court can now judge the fairness and justness of procedure established by law to deprive a person of his personal liberty. Just a semblance of procedure which is fanciful and arbitrary could not be valid. The Court also held that Articles 21,19 and 14 were interlinked and not mutually exclusive. The attempt of the Court will be to expand the ambit of the Fundamental Rights rather than to constrict it. The Court has thus re-interpreted Article 21 and overruled the verdict in Gopalan Case. J.Iyer had said, "The Spirit of man is at the root of Article 21, and personal liberty makes for the worth of the human person." J. Bhagwati said, "Article 21,.... embodies a constitutional value of supreme importance in a democratic society. The Court has specifically ruled that Article 14 outlaws unreasonableness and arbitrariness."

The word 'law' under Article 300-A, which was added while deleting Article 31 (44th Amendment), clearly indicates that the Parliament intended to confer on the citizens a right to hold property which could not be deprived without the authority of law (a legal right), in spite of deletion of Article 31 which placed a constitutional obligation to pay adequate compensation (as a fundamental right). Now the Court can interpret Article 300-A in a meaningful sense, with the same judicial approach which was adopted in the Maneka Gandhi Case. After Maneka Gandhi case the expression "authority of law" must mean "just, fair and reasonable" law, hence any legislation providing for deprivation of property under Article 300-A must be "just, fair and reasonable". This puts a premium on the whims and fancies of the majority based laws in Parliament where political climate rules with sentiments, and has an ever-changing fragile character.

All the above decisions ultimately restrict the power of our Parliament, making its position different from that of the British Parliament.

Certain Doctrines Regarding Judicial Review

During the course of constitutional interpretation by the Supreme Court a few doctrines have been evolved/adopted in India. These are briefly stated below.

Doctrine of Ultra Vires

The term *ultra vires* simply means powers or 'lack of power'.

An act is said to be *ultra vires* when it is in excess of power of the person or authority doing it. When a legislative enactment or any of its provisions are said to be *ultra vires* of the Constitution it means that the legislature which purported to enact it, exceeded the power conferred on it under the Constitution. When a rule is said to be *ultra vires* of the Act, it means that the authority which purported to make the rule, exceeded the power conferred upon it by the Act.

Ultra vires points to the capacity or power of the person to do that act. It is not necessary that an act to be *ultra vires* must also be illegal. It may be, but it may as well not be illegal, the essence of the doctrine of *ultra vires* is that the act is done in excess of the powers possessed by the person in law.

The doctrine of Judicial Review developed in the United States by their Supreme Court during the tenure of C.J. John Marshall was first enunciated by the learned Judge in Marbury vs. Madison in 1803. The Court argued that the Constitution seeks to define and limit the powers of the legislature and that there would be on purpose in doing so if the legislature could over step these limits at any time. In the words of the Court, "Certainly all those who framed the written constitutions contemplate them as fundamental and paramount law of the nation and consequently the theory of every such government must be that an Act of the legislature repugnant to the Constitution, is void." This doctrine has also been adopted in India and has the explicit sanction of the Indian Constitution (Articles 13, 32, 131-136, 143 and 226, 246).

It is during Judicial Review that the highest court may declare an Act of legislature or even an executive order as *ultra vires* of the Constitution.

Literal Construction

Literal Construction means literal interpretation of the laws or Constitution. The predominant approach of the Indian Judiciary was positivist i.e. to interpret the Constitution literally and to apply to it, more or less, the same restrictive canons of interpretations as are usually applied in case of ordinary statutes. The principle was to go by the plain words used by the Constitution makers. Art. 367 of the Constitution provides for the application of the General Clauses Act of 1897 which defines the scope for interpretation in case of general enactments. This Act can be amended by Parliament and as such the scope of interpretation under Article 367 can also be amended. The courts have told that not only the 'general definitions' under the said Act, but also the 'general rules of construction' in the Act apply to the Constitution. Thus, literal construction is a restricted or strict interpretation, the height of which was reached in the Gopalan Case. A broad interpretation takes into consideration the scope of the word not literally but from the 'spirit' of the word and other factors/ provisions as well the changing situations, ideologies etc. This view has been adopted by the United States Supreme Court while interpreting the U.S. Constitution. Later, in India, the decision on the Habeas Corpus case during emergency has been characterised as based on most narrow, restrictive and literal interpretation of the Constitution. While such views were taken in the above case as well as the Gopalan case, Supreme Court has also opined that in interpreting the Constituton the Judicial approach should be "dynamic rather than static, pragmatic and not pedantic and elastic rather than rigid" (Pathumma vs. Kerala, 1978; R.S. Joshi vs. Ajit Mills, 1977). Such interpretations have been given in Keshavanand Bharthi Case or the Maneka Gandhi Case. Keshavanand case has been regarded as the high-water mark of purposive interpretation of Constitution. With the Maneka Gandhi Case (in post-emergency era) the Supreme Court has breathed new vigour into the concept of personal liberty and given new dimensions to the right of equality.

Doctrine of Pith and Substance

Parliament or State legislature must legislate within the Constitutional limits defined by the three lists. Courts can declare legislation as bad and void if the limits are transgressed or encroached upon, but while doing so the Court applies the rule of pith and substance. This rule envisages that the legislation as a whole be examined to ascertain its true nature and character.

The rule has been borrowed from Canada. It means that to ascertain the true character of law, it must be looked into as an organic whole. The object should be taken in as one piece and then its true character determined, and not in a disintegrated part or as a more collection of reactions (e.g. Bombay Money Lenders Act—Prafulla Kumar vs. Bank of Commerce, Khulna).

This doctrine introduces a degree of flexibility into the otherwise rigid scheme of distribution of powers.

In Bombay vs. R.M.D.C. case, while considering the validity of the Bombay Lotteries and Prize Competitions Control and Tax (Amendment) Act, 1952 vis-a-vis Articles 19(1)(g) and 301, the Supreme Court pointed out that in pith and substance the impugned Act, was in respect of betting and gambling which do not constitute trade and commerce or business and hence valid.

The Doctrine of Colourable Legislation

The doctrine of colourable legislation is based on the maxim that what cannot be done directly, cannot also be done indirectly. The doctrine becomes applicable when a legislature seeks to do something in an indirect manner what it cannot do directly. Thus the doctrine refers to the question of legislative competence to enact a particular law. The Constitution distributes legislative powers between the Parliament and the State Legislatures and each has to act within its sphere. When the legislature transgresses the limits imposed on it by the Constitution, such transgression may be patent, manifest or direct or may be disguised, overt or indirect. It is to the latter class of cases that the expression 'colourable legislation' is applied. The idea is that although apparently the legislature purported to act within the limits of its powers, yet, in substance and in reality, transgressed these powers, in a veiled form, which, on proper examination, appears a pretence or disguise.

Colourable here means that which is *not* what it purports to be; or deceptive. Colourable is not tainted with bad faith or evil motive, it is not pejorative or crooked. Colourability is conceptually bound up with legislative incompetency.

Prospective Overruling

The doctrine of prospective overruling is associated with judicial review i.e. with the power of the Court to declare a law unconstitutional and void. Traditionally, a judicial declaration of a law as unconstitutional is deemed effective prospectively as well as retrospectively. An unconstitutional law is regarded as such since its inception. Thus this 'new' law is considered as having been there all the time even before the judgment of the court.

However, the Supreme Court of the United States developed a doctrine against this view which is known as the 'doctrine of prospective overruling'. The Court has in some cases taken a view that rather than disturbing the past transactions, the new view of the law adopted by the Court might be made effective as regards future transactions only. The doctrine envisages that a well established precedent may be overruled from a future date and not retrospectively.

By balancing all considerations the Court should decide whether the decision should be applied retrospectively or only prospectively. This doctrine overtly testifies to the law-making functions of the judiciary. In the Golaknath Case in India, five out of eleven Judges took recourse to the doctrine of prospective overruling. While declaring that the Parliament could not amend the fundamental rights, they declared this norm would operate only in future and not retrospectively. They also restricted it by stating that—

(i) This doctrine would be applied only by the Supreme Court and by no other Court;
(ii) Would be used only in Constitutional cases; and
(iii) Prospectively would be imposed only in Court's discretion in accordance with justice

In India, this doctrine has been applied in an extremely narrow area, and that too, to the invalidity of Constitutional amendments which were in force for a long time to form basis of mass of legislation affecting agrarian reforms. In the United States it indicated changes in judicial views as regards interpretations and scope of Constitutional provisions. While in the U.S. the theory was applied to the impugned law invalid from the date of the decision and not earlier, constitutional amendments were to remain valid forever, and principle of non-amendability of fundamental rights was to apply in future.

Judicial Activism

Judicial activism sounds to be a term of recent origin and has given rise to a controversy which is being discussed in India. It is considered to be a threat to the concept of separation of powers, considered sacred in modern democracies. However the seeds of judicial activism were sown in the land where Monte que's principle of separation of powers was first put into use by the fathers of the constitution though tempered by the concurrent principle of checks and balances. It was in the United States of America where in 1803, C.J. John Marshall delivered his historic judgment in Marbury vs. Madison and established the judicial supremacy in matters of the proper and judicious interpretation of the Constitution and its implied power to defend the Constitution against any encroachment by the Executive or the Legislature. This was the power to declare any executive order or legislative enactment as *ultra vires* (beyond law) and hence *void.* Though this was opposed by the other two branches, it was supported by the American people and has now become almost a basic characteristic of the American political system.

Usually we ascribe the origin of the doctrine of judicial review to Marbury Vs. Madison case in the United States. But in England in 1610 in the *Dr. Bonham's Case,* (8, Coke's Reports, 114 at 118) Lord Chief Justice Coke observed, "When an act of Parliament is against common law right and reason, or repugnant, or impossible to be performed, the common law will control it and adjudge such act to be void." Thus, 'state action' could be invalidated by reference to a higher organic instrument based on the natural law doctrine. But this doctrine did not become operational fully in England. Because of the conflict between the Crown and Parliament, judges sided with Parliament (may be because House of Lords—the highest Court—is a part of Parliament) and the theory of parliamentary sovereignty got established as against judicial supremacy. In modern times, even in Britain, Lord Denning, Lord Diplock etc. have emphasised the law-creative function of the judges and Lord Denning opined that the task of common law is to act as an instrument of evolution in accordance with the changing needs of the society and the demands of justice.

In India between 1950 upto 1980 the Courts had assumed the role of the protector of fundamental rights-sentinel of the people's rights. But later, it assumed the role of Saviour, and this role was supported by the people of India.

Analysing the situation of retired Judge observed, 'the three decades of the Republic brought the Indian society to an impasse where they found that the executive became impotent, because its political masters wanted it to be so. The legislature became devoid of teeth, because in it is the politicians who constitute the legislature. People in India got convinced that they would not get help either from the legislature or from the executive . . . . Two wings of the sovereignty became paralysed not because of their inherent defect, but because their political masters did want them to be paralysed for their (master's) political and personal benefits . . . . There was only one outlet open, and that is the Judiciary . . . . People reposed faith in judicial system because they had no other alternative.'[2]

C.J. Chandrachud, speaking for the Supreme Court had observed, 'It is really the poor, starved and mindless millions who need the Courts' protection for securing to themselves the enjoyment of human rights'. Justice Bhagwati, Justice Krishna Iyer, and Chief Justice Chandrachud were instrumental in uprooting the traditional doctrine of *locus standi* and opened the era of Public Interest Litigation. In exceptional cases, the Court declared, even a postcard sent by a poor helpless person sent to the court could be admitted as and petition for a writ. The scope and dimensions of public interest litigation went on increasing-quantitatively and varied issues and problems which should have and could have been solved either by an executive action or by legislative enactments came up before the Court and the courts applied their minds and passed orders. Disbelief in the executive reached such a dimension that the court had to pass an order that in a particular case the CBI will work under the direction of the Court and report straight to the Court and not to the Home Ministry.

Hundreds of cases, some being very minor were taken-up by High Courts and orders were issued to the executive to perform particular functions and report to the court. Traditional political scientists were baffled as they thought that the separation of powers and functions is in a jeopordy as the Judiciary is assuming the functions of the executive and the legislature is being belittled. But if one goes to the root and counts the number of scams, the declining standards of the discussions and debates in legislatures, one comes to the conclusion that judicial activism has come to stay as an inevitable development, a concesions to the weaknesses of our politicians who man our legislature and the executive.

Mr. P.N. Sangma, Speaker of Lok Sabha in an interview to Home TV on 14-04-1997 urged the political parties that, if the quality of debate in Parliament has to improve, if Parliament is to be conducted in an orderly manner then a major role has to be played by the respective political parties . . . . when they are giving nominations (of candidates for election) they should be very careful in choosing the candidates. He described the present method of political parties to nominate candidates as 'entirely wrong'. He further urged to build up their cadre and give same training before entering the election fray and expressed happiness at the BJP's starting refresher and training courses for its MPs and opined that though 'we also do it from Parliament side but we could not do much'. He urged the media to ignore the *hangamas* (pandemonium) in Parliament. This comment of the Honorable Speaker who has been maintaining the high dignity of the office is quite sufficient to show as to why the people are losing faith in their representatives and supporting judicial activism, which should not be allowed to reach a level of over activity due to the inoptitude of the legislature and of the executive which is a part of the legislature in our system.

REFERENCES

1. Joshi, G. N., 1983, The Constitution of India Macmillan India Ltd., p. 166.
2. Ratnaparkhi, M.S. (Retd. Justice) 'Is Judicial Activism—The only Alternative? II' *The Hitavada*, Nagpur, Dt. 23-03-1997.

BIBLIOGRAPHY

AIR—AIR-Relevant Volumes

Basu, Durga Das, 1992, *Introduction to the Constitution of India,* Prentice Hall of India, New Delhi.

Deogaonkar, S.G., 1993, *Bharatiya-Rajkiya Vyavastha* (Marathi), Shri Sainath Prakashan, Nagpur.

Government of India, *The Constitution of India* (Original Text).

Jain, M.P. 1993, *Indian Constitutional Law,* (4th Edition), N.M. Tripathi Pvt.Ltd. Bombay.

Joshi, G.N., 1983, *The Constitution of India* (Seventh Edition), Macmillan India Ltd. Delhi.

Pylee, M.V., 1965, *Constitutional Government in India,* Asia Pub. House, Bombay.

Lok Sabha Secretariat, 1985, *Rules of Procedure and Conduct of Business in Lok Sabha,* (Sixth Edition), Lok Sabha Secretariat, New Delhi.

Lok Sabha Secretariat, *Direction by the Speaker.*

INDEX